FAST
healthy

THE AUSTRALIAN
Women's Weekly

FAST
healthy

acp
books

contents

introduction	6
breakfast	10
juices	42
soups	98
snacks+light meals	114
salads	138
vegies+grains	190
seafood	214
chicken	282
meat	316
desserts	348
glossary	388
index	394
conversion chart	399

This book's aim is to show that cooking and eating healthily doesn't

have to take a lot of time or effort: enjoying how you cook and what

you eat are part and parcel of the whole process. It really is possible

to come up with a week's worth of uncomplicated but appealing meals

containing a wide array of foods that are unprocessed and fairly low

in fat — and get them on the table without a lot of fuss or frenzy.

Most of us who live an urban lifestyle crowd so much into our days that eating a healthy breakfast at home or cooking dinner after work on weeknights barely make it onto our list of priorities. In point of fact, eating well should come near the top of that list: the right diet, coupled with regular exercise, will help us maintain proper weight, aid in keeping our cholesterol and blood pressure levels under control and reduce the risk of heart disease and type-2 diabetes. And, of course, it also provides us with the energy and stamina required for our busy way of life.

A well-balanced breakfast, in particular, has been identified as an important habit to develop for a long and healthy life. After a food-free period of eight or more hours, the body and the brain both need fuel to kick-start them into action. People who skip breakfast generally have below average nutrition levels and are prone to catching more common illnesses, whereas breakfast-eaters have been found to have a lower daily fat intake, higher fibre intake, and significantly higher intakes of almost all vitamins and minerals. Skipping breakfast can result in mid-morning or lunchtime binges on high-sugar, high-fat fast foods. Nutritionists have found that people who eat a balanced breakfast concentrate better and are more efficient at work than those who skip it.

But who has the time to plan and prepare healthy meals? Well, you'll be happy to know that, with a little thought and a little trial and error on your part, you'll find that it doesn't take long nor is it difficult to eat a well-balanced breakfast or get a healthy meal on the table after work. In fact it's often quicker to cook at home than to buy pre-prepared and processed foods which still require a certain amount of handling and cooking before they're ready to eat.

There's an enormous array of foods you can select from for a balanced meal that doesn't take hours to make, and most are natural, wholesome and, in the main, chemical-free. It's important to eat as wide a range as possible, making certain to include many different wholegrains, breads and cereals, vegetables and fruits. With regard to the last two, think about eating something of every colour at dinner or from your lunch box to make it easy to consume the recommended five to nine daily servings. If you choose different colours — dark leafy greens, red or brown onions, cherry or teardrop tomatoes, blueberries, bectroot, papaya, orange juice and so on — you'll be eating healthily without thinking about it.

Getting a meal on the table after work when you're tired and hurried doesn't have to become an insurmoutable challenge. You want it to be healthy and taste good but you also want it to be fast and easy to prepare. In this cookbook, you'll find achievable and healthy mealtime solutions no matter how little time you have, and there are recipes here that everyone in the family will love. We're confident that you'll turn to this book constantly when making out your shopping list or planning meals that are as good tasting as they are good for you.

breakfast

Porridge with poached pears and blueberries

¾ cup (180ml) hot water
⅓ cup (30g) rolled oats
1 small pear (180g), cored, chopped coarsely
½ cup (125ml) cold water
2 tablespoons blueberries

1 Combine the hot water and oats in small saucepan over medium heat; cook, stirring, about 5 minutes or until porridge is thick and creamy.
2 Place pear and the cold water in small saucepan; bring to a boil. Reduce heat, simmer, uncovered, about 5 minutes or until pear softens.
3 Serve porridge topped with pears and 1 tablespoon of the poaching liquid; sprinkle with berries.

on the table in 20 minutes
serves 1 **per serving** 2.7g total fat (0.5g saturated fat); 882kJ (211 cal); 43.4g carbohydrate; 3.9g protein; 6.6g fibre

Baked ricotta with tomato

2 teaspoons olive oil
1 tablespoon pine nuts
2 cloves garlic, crushed
100g baby spinach leaves
1¼ cups (250g) low-fat ricotta cheese
1 egg, beaten lightly
2 tablespoons coarsely chopped fresh chives
500g baby vine-ripened truss tomatoes
1 tablespoon balsamic vinegar

1 Preheat oven to 220°C/200°C fan-forced. Oil four holes of a 6-hole (⅓ cup/80ml) muffin pan.
2 Heat half of the oil in medium frying pan; cook pine nuts and garlic until fragrant. Add spinach; stir until wilted. Cool 10 minutes.
3 Meanwhile, combine spinach mixture in medium bowl with cheese, egg and chives; divide among prepared holes. Bake about 15 minutes or until browned.
4 Combine tomatoes and vinegar with remaining oil in small shallow baking dish. Roast, uncovered, 10 minutes.
5 Serve baked ricotta with tomatoes.

on the table in 35 minutes
serves 4 **per serving** 11.8g total fat (4.4g saturated fat); 711kJ (170 cal); 4.2g carbohydrate; 10.6g protein; 2.7g fibre

Strawberry hotcakes with blueberry sauce

1 egg, separated
2 egg whites, extra
½ cup (125ml) apple sauce
1 teaspoon vanilla extract
2 cups (560g) low-fat yogurt
1¾ cups (280g) wholemeal self-raising flour
250g strawberries, hulled, chopped coarsely
blueberry sauce
150g blueberries, chopped coarsely
2 tablespoons white sugar
1 tablespoon water

1 Make blueberry sauce.
2 Using electric mixer, beat all egg whites in small bowl until soft peaks form. Combine egg yolk, apple sauce, extract, yogurt, flour and strawberries in large bowl; fold in egg whites.
3 Pour ¼ cup of the batter into heated large greased frying pan; using spatula, spread batter to shape into a round. Cook, over low heat, about 2 minutes or until bubbles appear on the surface. Turn hotcake; cook until lightly browned on other side. Remove from pan; cover to keep warm. Repeat with remaining batter.
4 Serve hotcakes with blueberry sauce.
blueberry sauce place ingredients in small saucepan; bring to a boil, stirring constantly. Reduce heat, simmer 2 minutes. Remove from heat; cool 10 minutes. Blend or process blueberry mixture until smooth.

on the table in 35 minutes
serves 4 **per serving** 2.6g total fat (0.7g saturated fat); 1814kJ (434 cal); 78.9g carbohydrate; 19.9g protein; 5.1g fibre

Sautéed mushrooms on toast

30g butter
200g swiss brown mushrooms, sliced thickly
100g fresh shiitake mushrooms
200g button mushrooms, halved
100g oyster mushrooms, halved
1 clove garlic, crushed
¼ cup (60ml) beef stock
½ loaf ciabatta bread (220g)
¼ cup coarsely chopped fresh flat-leaf parsley
¼ cup coarsely chopped fresh chives

1 Preheat grill.
2 Melt butter in large frying pan; cook mushrooms and garlic, stirring, about 5 minutes. Add stock; bring to a boil. Reduce heat, simmer, uncovered, about 10 minutes or until mushrooms are cooked as desired.
3 Meanwhile, trim end from bread; cut into eight slices. Toast bread both sides; divide among serving plates.
4 Stir herbs into mushrooms; serve on toast.

on the table in 30 minutes
serves 4 **per serving** 8.1g total fat (4.3g saturated fat); 966kJ (231 cal); 29.7g carbohydrate; 9.8g protein; 6.2g fibre

Breakfast with the lot

2 large egg tomatoes (180g), quartered
4 eggs
4 slices multigrain bread
60g light ham
50g baby spinach leaves

1 Preheat oven to 220°C/200°C fan-forced. Line oven tray with
baking paper.
2 Place tomato, cut-side up, on tray; roast, uncovered, about 25 minutes
or until softened and lightly browned.
3 Meanwhile place enough water in large shallow frying pan to come
halfway up the side; bring to a boil.
4 Break eggs, one at a time, into small bowl, sliding each into pan; allow
water to return to a boil. Cover pan, turn off heat; stand about 4 minutes
or until a light film of egg white has set over yolks.
5 Toast bread slices until lightly browned both sides.
6 Using an egg slide, remove eggs, one at a time, from pan; place egg,
still on slide, on absorbent paper-lined saucer to blot up any poaching
liquid. Serve toast topped with ham, spinach, egg then tomato.

on the table in 35 minutes
serves 4 **per serving** 6.7g total fat (1.9g saturated fat); 702kJ (168 cal);
13.0g carbohydrate; 12.8g protein; 2.2g fibre

Citrus compote

2 large limes (160g)
3 large oranges (900g)
2 medium pink grapefruit (850g)
2 teaspoons white sugar
½ vanilla bean, split lengthways
1 tablespoon small fresh mint leaves

1 Grate the rind of 1 lime and 1 orange finely; reserve grated rind.
Peel remaining lime, remaining oranges, and grapefruit.
2 Segment all citrus over a large bowl to save juice, removing and
discarding membrane from each segment. Add segments to bowl
with sugar, vanilla bean and reserved rind; stir gently to combine.
3 Stand, covered, at room temperature 10 minutes; sprinkle with
mint leaves.

on the table in 30 minutes
serves 4 **per serving** 0.5g total fat (0.0g saturated fat); 485kJ (116 cal);
22.0g carbohydrate; 3.2g protein; 4.6g fibre

Crisp prosciutto with mango and avocado salsa

1 medium mango (430g), chopped coarsely
1 large avocado (320g), chopped coarsely
1 small red onion (100g), chopped finely
1 small red capsicum (150g), chopped finely
1 fresh small red thai chilli, chopped finely
2 tablespoons lime juice
8 slices prosciutto (120g), halved lengthways

1 Place mango, avocado, onion, capsicum, chilli and juice in medium bowl; toss salsa to combine.
2 Cook prosciutto in large oiled frying pan until crisp.
3 Serve prosciutto with salsa.

on the table in 25 minutes
serves 4 **per serving** 14.7g total fat (3.4g saturated fat); 920kJ (220 cal); 12.7g carbohydrate; 8.2g protein; 2.7g fibre

Morning trifles

⅓ cup (20g) all-bran
⅓ cup (20g) special k
⅓ cup (20g) puffed wheat
250g strawberries, hulled
1 cup (280g) low-fat vanilla yogurt
⅓ cup (80ml) passionfruit pulp

1 Combine cereals in small bowl.
2 Cut six strawberries in half; reserve. Slice remaining strawberries thinly.
3 Divide half of the cereal mixture among four 1-cup (250ml) serving bowls; divide half of the yogurt, all the strawberry slices and half of the passionfruit pulp among bowls. Continue layering with remaining cereal and yogurt; top with reserved strawberry halves and remaining passionfruit pulp.

on the table in 20 minutes
serves 4 **per serving** 0.7g total fat (0.1g saturated fat); 543kJ (130 cal); 19.0g carbohydrate; 8.3g protein; 7.2g fibre
tip you will need about 5 passionfruit for this recipe.

Poached eggs with bacon, spinach and pecorino

600g spinach, trimmed, chopped coarsely
4 rashers rindless bacon (250g)
4 eggs
⅓ cup (40g) pecorino cheese flakes

1 Boil, steam or microwave spinach until just wilted; drain. Cover to keep warm.
2 Heat large frying pan; cook bacon until crisp. Drain on absorbent paper; cover to keep warm.
3 Half-fill the same pan with water; bring to a boil. Break eggs one at a time into small bowl; slide into pan. When all eggs are in pan, allow water to return to a boil. Cover pan, turn off heat; stand about 4 minutes or until a light film of egg white sets over yolks. Using an egg slide, remove eggs, one at a time from pan; place on absorbent paper-lined saucer to blot up poaching liquid.
4 Divide spinach among serving plates; top each spinach portion with bacon, egg then cheese.

on the table in 15 minutes
serves 4 **per serving** 10.5g total fat (4.1g saturated fat); 794kJ (190 cal); 1.2g carbohydrate; 20.9g protein; 4.1g fibre

Untoasted muesli

2 cups (180g) rolled oats
½ cup (35g) all-bran
1 tablespoon sunflower seed kernels
⅓ cup (55g) sultanas
¼ cup (35g) finely chopped dried apricots
½ cup (80g) finely chopped seeded dried dates
3 cups (750ml) no-fat milk
½ cup (140g) low-fat yogurt

1 Combine oats, all-bran, kernels and dried fruit in large bowl.
2 Divide muesli and milk among serving bowls. Top with yogurt.

on the table in 10 minutes
serves 6 **per serving** 4.8g total fat (0.8g saturated fat); 1204kJ
(288 cal); 45.4g carbohydrate; 11.7g protein; 7.3g fibre
tip you can use fruit juice, such as apple, instead of the milk, if you like.

Bruschetta with smoked salmon, cream cheese and rocket

⅓ cup (80g) light cream cheese
1 shallot (25g), chopped finely
2 teaspoons lemon juice
½ teaspoon dijon mustard
1 tablespoon drained capers, rinsed, chopped coarsely
1 loaf sourdough bread (675g)
30g baby rocket leaves
200g sliced smoked salmon

1 Preheat grill.
2 Combine cream cheese, shallot, juice, mustard and capers in small bowl.
3 Trim ends from bread, cut into eight slices. Toast bread both sides. Spread cheese mixture over toast; divide among plates. Top with rocket and salmon.

on the table in 20 minutes
serves 4 **per serving** 10.1g total fat (3.3g saturated fat) 2153kJ (515 cal) 77.1g carbohydrate 28g protein 8g fibre

Scrambled eggs with dill and smoked salmon

7 eggs
½ cup (125ml) no-fat milk
1 tablespoon finely chopped fresh dill
10g butter
300g thinly sliced smoked salmon

1 Whisk eggs in medium bowl; add milk and dill, whisk until combined.
2 Melt butter in medium frying pan; cook egg mixture over low heat, stirring gently, until mixture is just set.
3 Serve egg mixture with salmon.

on the table in 15 minutes
serves 4 **per serving** 14.7g total fat (4.9g saturated fat); 1087kJ (260 cal); 1.9g carbohydrate; 30.1g protein; 0.0g fibre

Bruschetta with strawberry, banana and ricotta

½ loaf ciabatta bread (220g)
200g low-fat ricotta cheese
2 tablespoons honey
1 teaspoon finely grated orange rind
¼ teaspoon ground cinnamon
125g strawberries, sliced thickly
1 small banana (130g), sliced thinly
2 tablespoons brown sugar

1 Preheat grill.
2 Trim ends from bread; cut into eight slices.
3 Beat ricotta, honey, rind and cinnamon in small bowl with electric mixer until smooth.
4 Combine strawberries, banana and sugar in small frying pan; stir gently over low heat until sugar dissolves.
5 Toast bread both sides. Spread with ricotta mixture, divide among plates; top with strawberry mixture.

on the table in 25 minutes
serves 4 **per serving** 5.8g total fat (3g saturated fat); 1208kJ (289 cal); 49g carbohydrate; 10.8g protein; 2.8g fibre

Egg-white omelette

150g light ham
200g button mushrooms, sliced thinly
12 egg whites
¼ cup finely chopped fresh chives
2 medium tomatoes (380g), chopped coarsely
½ cup (45g) coarsely grated low-fat cheddar cheese
8 slices wholemeal bread

1 Trim and discard any fat from ham; cut into thin strips. Cook ham in heated large frying pan, stirring, until lightly browned. Remove from pan. Cook mushrooms in same pan, stirring, until lightly browned.
2 Using electric mixer, beat 3 of the egg whites in small bowl until soft peaks form; fold in a quarter of the chives. Preheat grill.
3 Pour egg-white mixture into heated oiled 20cm frying pan; cook, uncovered, over low heat until just browned underneath. Place pan under grill; cook until top just sets. Place a quarter of the tomato on one half of the omelette; return to grill, cook until tomato is hot and top is lightly browned. Gently place a quarter of each of the cheese, ham and mushroom on tomato half of omelette; fold over to enclose filling. Carefully transfer omelette to serving plate; cover to keep warm.
4 Repeat step 2 with remaining egg whites, chives and fillings.
5 Toast bread until lightly browned both sides; serve with omelettes.

on the table in 25 minutes
serves 4 **per serving** 4.0g total fat (1.2g saturated fat); 1032kJ (247 cal); 23.5g carbohydrate; 25.8g protein; 6.0g fibre

Pancetta and eggs

8 slices pancetta (120g)
2 green onions, chopped coarsely
4 eggs
4 thick slices white bread

1 Preheat oven to 200°C/180°C fan-forced. Oil four holes of 12-hole
(⅓ cup/80ml) muffin pan.
2 Line holes with 2 slices of the pancetta, overlapping to form cup shape.
Divide onion among pancetta cups; break one egg into each pancetta cup.
3 Bake, uncovered, about 10 minutes or until eggs are just cooked and
pancetta is crisp around edges. Remove from pan carefully.
4 Toast bread until lightly browned both sides. Serve pancetta and eggs
on toast.

on the table in 20 minutes
serves 4 **per serving** 10.1g total fat (3.3g saturated fat); 853kJ
(204 cal); 13.1g carbohydrate; 14.9g protein; 0.9g fibre

juices

Peach, apple and strawberry

1 medium apple (150g), cut into wedges
1 medium peach (150g), cut into wedges
2 strawberries (40g)

1 Push ingredients through juice extractor into glass; stir to combine.

on the table in 5 minutes
serves 1 **per serving** 0.3g total fat (0g saturated fat); 451kJ (108 cal);
24.3g carbohydrate; 2.2g protein; 5.1g fibre
tip we used a green apple in this recipe, but you can use the colour of
your choice.

Mixed berry

3 strawberries (60g)
¼ cup (40g) blueberries
¼ cup (35g) raspberries
⅓ cup (80ml) water

1 Blend or process ingredients until smooth; pour into glass.

on the table in 5 minutes
serves 1 **per serving** 0.2g total fat (0.0g saturated fat); 209kJ (50 cal);
8.2g carbohydrate; 1.7g protein; 3.9g fibre
tip for something refreshing, freeze the juice until almost set then scrape
with a fork for a granita-like snack.

Grapefruit and blood orange

2 small blood oranges (360g)
1 small grapefruit (350g)

1 Juice oranges and grapefruit on citrus squeezer; pour into glass.

on the table in 5 minutes
serves 1 **per serving** 0.7g total fat (0g saturated fat); 652kJ (156 cal);
31.2g carbohydrate; 4.6g protein; 6.5g fibre

Orange and ginger

3 medium oranges (720g)
2cm piece fresh ginger (10g), grated

1 Juice oranges on citrus squeezer; pour into glass.
2 Stir in ginger.

on the table in 5 minutes
serves 1 **per serving** 0.6g total fat (0g saturated fat); 807kJ (193 cal);
40.9g carbohydrate; 5.2g protcin; 10.5g fibre

Tangelo and ginger

2 medium tangelos (420g)
2cm piece fresh ginger (10g), grated

1 Juice tangelos on citrus squeezer; pour into glass.
2 Stir in ginger.

on the table in 5 minutes
serves 1 **per serving** 0.3g total fat (0g saturated fat); 477kJ (114 cal);
23.7g carbohydrate; 1.9g protein; 6.2g fibre

Watercress, beetroot and celery

1 trimmed celery stalk (100g), chopped coarsely
3 baby beetroots (75g), cut into wedges
50g watercress, trimmed
½ cup (125ml) water

1 Push celery, beetroot and watercress through juice extractor into glass.
2 Stir in the water.

on the table in 5 minutes
serves 1 **per serving** 0.4g total fat (0g saturated fat); 222kJ (53 cal);
8.9g carbohydrate; 3.5g protein; 6g fibre

Watermelon and mint

450g watermelon
3 fresh mint leaves

1 Blend or process ingredients until smooth; pour into glass.

on the table in 5 minutes
serves 1 **per serving** 0.6g total fat (0g saturated fat); 280kJ (67 cal);
14.5g carbohydrate; 0.9g protein; 1.9g fibre

Carrot, ginger and silverbeet

2 medium carrots (240g), chopped coarsely
3 trimmed silverbeet leaves (240g), chopped coarsely
2cm piece fresh ginger (10g)

1 Push ingredients through juice extractor into glass; stir to combine.

on the table in 5 minutes
serves 1 **per serving** 0.7g total fat (0g saturated fat); 364kJ (87 cal);
14.5g carbohydrate; 5.4g protein; 13.1g fibre

Beetroot, carrot and spinach

1 small beetroot (100g), cut into wedges
1 small carrot (70g), chopped coarsely
20g baby spinach leaves
½ cup (125ml) water

1 Push beetroot, carrot and spinach through juice extractor into glass.
2 Stir in the water.

on the table in 5 minutes
serves 1 **per serving** 0.2g total fat (0g saturated fat); 238kJ (57 cal);
11.2g carbohydrate; 2.7g protein; 5.3g fibre

Pineapple, ginger and mint

You will need ½ small pineapple for this recipe.

400g pineapple, chopped coarsely
1 cup firmly packed fresh mint leaves
1cm piece fresh ginger (5g)

1 Push ingredients through juice extractor into glass; stir to combine.

on the table in 5 minutes
serves 1 **per serving** 0.8g total fat (0.1g saturated fat); 418kJ (100 cal);
19.1g carbohydrate; 3.7g protein; 8.1g fibre

Apple and pear

1 medium apple (150g), cut into wedges
1 medium pear (230g), cut into wedges

1 Push ingredients through juice extractor into glass; stir to combine.

on the table in 5 minutes
serves 1 **per serving** 0.4g total fat (0g saturated fat); 853kJ (204 cal);
51.3g carbohydrate; 1.1g protein; 9g fibre
tip we used a green apple in this recipe, but you can use the colour of
your choice.

Orange, carrot and celery

1 large orange (300g), peeled, quartered
1 large carrot (180g), chopped coarsely
1 trimmed celery stalk (100g), chopped coarsely

1 Push orange, carrot and celery through juice extractor into glass; stir to combine.

on the table in 5 minutes
serves 1 **per serving** 0.5g total fat (0g saturated fat); 573kJ (137 cal); 28.6g carbohydrate; 4.2g protein; 11.3g fibre

Mango and grapefruit

1 small grapefruit (350g)
1 small mango (300g), chopped coarsely
¼ cup (60ml) water

1 Juice grapefruit on citrus squeezer; pour into glass.
2 Blend or process mango and the water until smooth. Transfer to same glass; stir to combine.

on the table in 5 minutes
serves 1 **per serving** 0.9g total fat (0g saturated fat); 757kJ (181 cal); 37.8g carbohydrate; 4.2g protein; 4.6g fibre

Mandarin

3 small mandarins (300g)

1 Juice mandarins on citrus squeezer; pour into glass.

on the table in 5 minutes
serves 1 **per serving** 0.4g total fat (0g saturated fat); 343kJ (82 cal);
17g carbohydrate; 1.9g protein; 4.3g fibre

Pear and grape

1 medium pear (230g), cut into wedges
175g seedless red grapes

1 Push ingredients through juice extractor into glass; stir to combine.

on the table in 5 minutes
serves 1 **per serving** 0.4g total fat (0g saturated fat); 953kJ (228 cal);
55.6g carbohydrate; 2.8g protein; 7.3g fibre

Pineapple, orange and strawberry

1 small orange (180g), peeled, quartered
150g pineapple, chopped coarsely
2 strawberries (40g)
¼ cup (60ml) water

1 Push orange, pineapple and strawberries through juice extractor into glass; stir in the water.

on the table in 5 minutes
serves 1 **per serving** 0.3g total fat (0g saturated fat); 468kJ (112 cal); 23.2g carbohydrate; 3.5g protein; 6.6g fibre

Ginger, orange and pineapple

You will need ¼ small pineapple for this recipe.

1 medium orange (240g)
200g pineapple, chopped coarsely
2cm piece fresh ginger (10g)

1 Juice orange on citrus squeezer; pour into glass.
2 Blend or process pineapple and ginger until smooth. Stir into orange juice.

on the table in 5 minutes
serves 1 **per serving** 0.3g total fat (0g saturated fat); 439kJ (105 cal);
22.2g carbohydrate; 2.8g protein; 5.9g fibre

Pear and ginger

2 medium pears (460g), cut into wedges
2cm piece fresh ginger (10g)

1 Push ingredients through juice extractor into glass; stir to combine.

on the table in 5 minutes
serves 1 **per serving** 0.5g total fat (0g saturated fat); 882kJ (211 cal);
52.6g carbohydrate; 1.3g protein; 9.8g fibre

Raspberry and peach

1 large peach (220g), chopped coarsely
¼ cup (35g) raspberries
½ cup (125ml) water

1 Blend or process peach and raspberry until smooth; pour into glass.
2 Stir in the water.

on the table in 5 minutes
serves 1 **per serving** 0.3g total fat (0g saturated fat); 301kJ (72 cal); 14.1g carbohydrate; 2.1g protein; 4.5g fibre

Silverbeet, apple and celery

1 trimmed silverbeet leaf (80g), chopped coarsely
1 large apple (200g), cut into wedges
1 trimmed celery stalk (100g), chopped coarsely

1 Push ingredients through juice extractor into glass; stir to combine.

on the table in 5 minutes
serves 1 **per serving** 0.5g total fat (0g saturated fat); 460kJ (110 cal); 24.6g carbohydrate; 2.4g protein; 7.8g fibre
tip we used a green apple in this recipe, but you can use the colour of your choice.

Strawberry and papaya

4 strawberries (80g)
80g papaya
½ cup (125ml) water

1 Blend or process ingredients until smooth; pour into glass.

on the table in 5 minutes
serves 1 **per serving** 0.2g total fat (0g saturated fat); 163kJ (39 cal);
7.7g carbohydrate; 1.7g protein; 3.6g fibre
tips we used the red-fleshed hawaiian or fijian variety of papaya in this
recipe. For something refreshing, freeze the juice until almost set then
scrape with a fork for a granita-like snack.

Apple and celery

2 small apples (260g), cut into wedges
1 trimmed celery stalk (100g), chopped coarsely

1 Push ingredients through juice extractor into glass; stir to combine.

on the table in 5 minutes
serves 1 **per serving** 0.4g total fat (0g saturated fat); 598kJ (143 cal);
34.7g carbohydrate; 1.4g protein; 7g fibre
tip we used green apples in this recipe, but you can use the colour of
your choice.

Orange, mango and strawberry

2 small oranges (360g)
1 small mango (300g), chopped coarsely
3 strawberries (60g), chopped coarsely

1 Juice oranges on citrus squeezer; pour into glass.
2 Blend or process mango and strawberries until smooth; stir into orange juice.

on the table in 5 minutes
serves 1 **per serving** 0.7g total fat (0g saturated fat); 949kJ (227 cal); 48.7g carbohydrate; 5.7g protein; 9.6g fibre

Kiwi fruit and green grape

3 medium kiwi fruits (255g), quartered
70g seedless green grapes
¼ cup (60ml) water

1 Blend or process ingredients until smooth; pour into glass.

on the table in 5 minutes
serves 1 **per serving** 0.5g total fat (0g saturated fat); 623kJ (149 cal);
31.8g carbohydrate; 3.5g protein; 7.8g fibre

Banana soy smoothie

1 cup (250ml) soy milk
1 small banana (130g), chopped coarsely

1 Blend or process ingredients until smooth; pour into glass.

on the table in 5 minutes
serves 1 **per serving** 2.1g total fat (0.2g saturated fat); 255kJ (61 cal);
8.2g carbohydrate; 8.2g protein; 0.9g fibre

Strawberry, honey and soy smoothie

6 strawberries (120g)
½ cup (125ml) soy milk
1 teaspoon honey

1 Blend or process ingredients until smooth; pour into glass.

on the table in 5 minutes
serves 1 **per serving** 3.6g total fat (0.4g saturated fat); 472kJ (113 cal); 14.4g carbohydrate; 6.2g protein; 3.2g fibre

Orange, carrot and ginger

2 medium oranges (480g), peeled, quartered
1 small carrot (70g), chopped coarsely
2cm piece fresh ginger (10g)

1 Push orange, carrot and ginger through juice extractor into glass;
stir to combine.

on the table in 5 minutes
serves 1 **per serving** 0.4g total fat (0g saturated fat); 606kJ (145 cal);
30.6g carbohydrate; 4g protein; 8.8g fibre

soups

Clear vegetable soup

2 litres (8 cups) vegetable stock
4 trimmed corn cobs (1kg)
2 cups (200g) coarsely chopped cauliflower
2 small carrots (140g), cut into 1cm pieces
120g snow peas, trimmed, sliced thinly
4 green onions, sliced thinly

1 Bring stock to a boil in large saucepan.
2 Cut kernels from corn cob, add to pan with cauliflower and carrot; return to a boil. Reduce heat, simmer, covered, about 10 minutes or until cauliflower is just tender.
3 Stir in snow peas and onion; simmer, uncovered, 2 minutes.

on the table in 30 minutes
serves 4 **per serving** 4.4g total fat (1.2g saturated fat); 1162kJ (278 cal); 38.1g carbohydrate; 15.6g protein; 10.8g fibre

Chicken pho

You will need to purchase a large barbecued chicken weighing about 900g for this recipe.

1.5 litres (6 cups) chicken stock
2cm piece fresh ginger (10g), grated finely
1 clove garlic, crushed
¼ cup (60ml) fish sauce
10cm stick (20g) finely chopped fresh lemon grass
1 teaspoon sambal oelek
4 green onions, sliced thinly
100g dried rice stick noodles
3 cups (480g) shredded cooked chicken
1 cup (80g) bean sprouts
½ cup firmly packed fresh mint leaves
2 tablespoons finely chopped fresh coriander

1 Combine stock, ginger, garlic, sauce and lemon grass in large saucepan; bring to a boil. Reduce heat, simmer, covered, 8 minutes. Remove from heat; stir in sambal oelek and onion.
2 Meanwhile place noodles in medium heatproof bowl; cover with boiling water. Stand until just tender; drain.
3 Divide noodles among serving bowls; top with chicken. Ladle soup over chicken; top with sprouts, mint and coriander.

on the table in 30 minutes
serves 4 **per serving** 9.0g total fat (2.8g saturated fat); 1204kJ (288 cal); 18.4g carbohydrate; 32.4g protein; 2.1g fibre

Leek and potato soup

1 tablespoon olive oil
2 cloves garlic, crushed
2 teaspoons fresh thyme leaves
4 small leeks (800g), sliced thinly
4 medium potatoes (800g), chopped coarsely
2 litres (8 cups) vegetable stock
2 green onions, sliced thinly

1 Heat oil in large saucepan; cook garlic, thyme and leek, stirring, about
3 minutes or until leek softens. Add potato and stock; bring to a boil.
Reduce heat, simmer, covered, about 15 minutes or until potato is tender.
2 Blend or process leek mixture until smooth.
3 Reheat soup; serve soup topped with onion.

on the table in 35 minutes
serves 4 **per serving** 7.3g total fat (1.7g saturated fat); 1058kJ (253 cal);
30.9g carbohydrate; 12.3g protein; 6.6g fibre

Curried chicken and zucchini soup

1 tablespoon low-fat dairy-free spread
1 medium brown onion (150g), chopped finely
1 clove garlic, crushed
1 teaspoon curry powder
½ cup (100g) doongara rice
340g chicken breast fillets, sliced thinly
2 cups (500ml) water
1 litre (4 cups) chicken stock
4 medium zucchini (480g), grated coarsely

1 Melt spread in large saucepan; cook onion and garlic, stirring, until onion softens. Add curry powder; cook, stirring, until mixture is fragrant.
2 Add rice and chicken; cook, stirring, 2 minutes. Add the water and stock; bring to a boil. Reduce heat, simmer, covered, 10 minutes. Add zucchini; cook, stirring, 5 minutes or until chicken is cooked through.

on the table in 35 minutes
serves 4 **per serving** 5.4g total fat (1.4g saturated fat); 1087kJ (260 cal); 25.6g carbohydrate; 25.7g protein; 2.7g fibre
tip doongara, the aboriginal word for white lightning, is a gluten-free rice that can be found at your local supermarket.

Meatball pho

400g lean beef mince
2 x 10cm sticks (40g) finely chopped fresh lemon grass
2 green onions, chopped finely
1 clove garlic, crushed
1 egg white
1.5 litres (6 cups) beef stock
2 star anise
1 stick cinnamon
185g dried rice stick noodles
1 cup (80g) bean sprouts
1 cup loosely packed fresh coriander leaves
2 fresh long red chillies, sliced thinly
4 green onions, sliced thinly

1 Using hand, combine beef, lemon grass, chopped onion, garlic and egg white in medium bowl; roll level tablespoons of the mixture into balls.
2 Meanwhile, place stock, star anise and cinnamon in large saucepan; bring to a boil. Reduce heat, simmer, uncovered, 5 minutes. Add meatballs; return to a boil. Reduce heat, simmer, uncovered, about 5 minutes or until meatballs are cooked through. Discard star anise and cinnamon from pan.
3 Place noodles in large heatproof bowl, cover with boiling water, stand until just tender; drain.
4 Divide noodles, meatballs and stock among serving bowls; top with combined sprouts, coriander, chilli and sliced onion. Serve with lime wedges, if desired.

on the table in 35 minutes
serves 4 **per serving** 7.2g total fat (2.9g saturated fat); 1267kJ (303 cal); 28.2g carbohydrate; 29.9g protein; 1.7g fibre

Ginger vegetable and soba soup

2 litres (8 cups) vegetable stock
1 tablespoon tamari
20cm piece fresh ginger (100g), grated
3 cloves garlic, crushed
4 small carrots (280g), cut into matchsticks
200g snow peas, trimmed, sliced thinly lengthways
200g dried soba noodles

1 Combine stock, tamari, ginger and garlic in large saucepan; bring to a boil. Reduce heat, simmer, covered, 5 minutes. Add carrot and snow peas; simmer, uncovered, about 3 minutes or until carrot is tender.
2 Cook noodles in small saucepan of boiling water, uncovered, until just tender; drain.
3 Place noodles in serving bowl; ladle soup over noodles.

on the table in 35 minutes
serves 4 **per serving** 2.9g total fat (1.1g saturated fat); 1145kJ (274 cal); 44.6g carbohydrate; 13.7g protein; 5.5g fibre
tip soba is a Japanese noodle, similar in appearance to spaghetti, made from buckwheat.

Tom yum goong

16 uncooked medium king prawns (720g)
1 tablespoon peanut oil
10cm stick (20g) finely chopped fresh lemon grass
2 cloves garlic, crushed
4cm piece fresh ginger (20g), grated
1.125 litres (4½ cups) fish stock
3 cups (750ml) water
3 fresh small red thai chillies, sliced thinly
2 fresh kaffir lime leaves, shredded finely
¼ cup (60ml) fish sauce
⅓ cup (80ml) lime juice
4 green onions, sliced thinly
¼ cup loosely packed fresh coriander leaves
¼ cup loosely packed fresh thai basil leaves

1 Shell and devein prawns, leaving tails intact; reserve prawn heads and shells.
2 Heat oil in large saucepan; cook reserved prawn heads and shells, stirring, about 3 minutes or until heads and shells are deep orange in colour. Add lemon grass, garlic and ginger; cook, stirring, until fragrant.
3 Stir in stock, the water, chilli and lime leaves; bring to a boil. Reduce heat, simmer, uncovered, 10 minutes. Strain stock through muslin-lined sieve into large heatproof bowl; discard solids.
4 Return stock to same cleaned pan; bring to a boil. Add prawns; reduce heat, simmer, uncovered, until prawns are changed in colour. Remove from heat; stir in sauce and juice. Serve soup sprinkled with onion and herbs.

on the table in 35 minutes
serves 4 **per serving** 5.9g total fat (1g saturated fat); 686kJ (164 cal); 3.6g carbohydrate; 23.2g protein; 1.1g fibre

snacks+
light meals

Lavash wrap

1 slice wholemeal lavash
¼ small avocado (50g)
1 teaspoon tahini
½ cup (60g) coarsely grated uncooked beetroot
⅓ cup (50g) coarsely grated uncooked pumpkin
¼ small red capsicum (40g), sliced thinly
40g button mushrooms, sliced thinly
¼ small red onion (25g), sliced thinly

1 Spread bread with avocado and tahini.
2 Place remaining ingredients on long side of bread; roll to enclose filling, cut in half.

on the table in 15 minutes
serves 1 **per serving** 13.4g total fat (2.6g saturated fat); 1463kJ
(350 cal); 45.1g carbohydrate; 12.2g protein; 10.1g fibre

Pan-fried haloumi with green salad

150g curly endive
50g baby spinach leaves
½ cup loosely packed fresh flat-leaf parsley leaves
⅔ cup (125g) drained semi-dried tomatoes, chopped coarsely
250g haloumi cheese
lemon dijon dressing
¼ cup (60ml) lemon juice
1 clove garlic, crushed
1 tablespoon water
1 teaspoon white sugar
1 teaspoon dijon mustard
¼ teaspoon ground cumin
pinch cayenne pepper

1 Make lemon dijon dressing.
2 Place endive, spinach, parsley and tomato in medium bowl with dressing; toss gently to combine.
3 Cut cheese into eight slices. Cook cheese in heated oiled medium frying pan, in batches, until browned both sides.
4 Serve salad topped with cheese.
lemon dijon dressing place ingredients in screw-top jar; shake well.

on the table in 20 minutes
serves 4 **per serving** 12g fat (7g saturated fat); 949kJ (227 cal); 11.8g carbohydrate; 17.3g protein; 5.4g fibre
tip haloumi must be cooked just before serving or it becomes leathery and unpalatable.

Gourmet chicken sandwiches

600g chicken breast fillets
2 cups (500ml) chicken stock
1½ cups (375ml) water
⅓ cup (50g) drained sun-dried tomatoes
1 tablespoon coarsely chopped fresh rosemary
2 tablespoons chicken stock, extra
½ long loaf turkish bread
½ small red onion (50g), sliced thinly
1 lebanese cucumber (130g), sliced thinly
60g baby rocket leaves
⅓ cup (95g) low-fat yogurt
½ teaspoon toasted black cumin seeds

1 Place chicken, stock and the water in large saucepan; bring to a boil. Reduce heat, simmer, uncovered, about 10 minutes or until cooked through. Cool chicken in poaching liquid 10 minutes. Remove chicken from pan; discard poaching liquid (or reserve for another use). Slice chicken thinly.
2 Drain tomatoes on absorbent paper; pressing firmly to remove as much oil as possible. Quarter tomatoes; blend or process with rosemary and extra stock until tomato mixture forms a paste.
3 Halve bread, slice pieces horizontally; toast both sides. Spread cut sides of bread with tomato paste; top with chicken, onion, cucumber and rocket. Serve with combined yogurt and seeds.

on the table in 35 minutes
serves 4 **per serving** 5.8g total fat (1.4g saturated fat); 1317kJ (315 cal); 21.8g carbohydrate; 41.6g protein; 3.4g fibre
tip black cumin seeds, also sold as jeera kala, are darker and sweeter than ordinary cumin and are sometimes confused with kalonji (nigella seeds). Used extensively in indian and moroccan-style cooking, the nutty flavour of black cumin seeds is brought out by toasting.

Garlic prawns and buk choy with herbed rice

36 uncooked medium prawns (1kg)
6 cloves garlic, crushed
2 teaspoons finely chopped fresh coriander
3 fresh small red thai chillies, chopped finely
⅓ cup (80ml) lime juice
1 teaspoon white sugar
1 tablespoon peanut oil
1kg baby buk choy, quartered lengthways
6 green onions, sliced thinly
1 tablespoon sweet chilli sauce
herbed rice
2 cups (400g) jasmine rice
2 tablespoons coarsely chopped fresh coriander
1 tablespoon coarsely chopped fresh mint
1 tablespoon coarsely chopped fresh flat-leaf parsley
1 teaspoon finely grated lime rind

1 Make herbed rice.
2 Shell and devein prawns, leaving tails intact.
3 Combine prawns in large bowl with garlic, coriander, chilli, juice and sugar.
4 Heat half of the oil in wok; stir-fry prawns, in batches, until just changed in colour.
5 Heat remaining oil with pan liquids in wok; stir-fry buk choy, onion and sauce, in batches, until just tender.
6 Return buk choy mixture and prawns to wok; stir-fry until hot. Serve on herbed rice.
herbed rice cook rice, uncovered, in large saucepan of boiling water until tender; drain. Return rice to pan; combine with remaining ingredients.

on the table in 35 minutes
serves 6 **per serving** 4.4g total fat (0.7g saturated fat); 1563kJ (374 cal); 56.7g carbohydrate; 23.9g protein; 3.7g fibre

Light-white frittata

You will need 200g of fresh peas in their pods for this recipe.

½ cup (80g) fresh shelled peas
1 medium yellow capsicum (200g), sliced thinly
1 small kumara (250g), grated coarsely
12 egg whites
½ cup (120g) light sour cream
1 cup loosely packed fresh basil leaves
¼ cup (20g) finely grated parmesan cheese

1 Preheat grill.
2 Cook peas, capsicum and kumara in heated lightly oiled 20cm frying pan, stirring, until just tender.
3 Meanwhile, whisk egg whites and cream in medium bowl; stir in basil.
4 Pour egg-white mixture over vegetables; cook, covered, over low heat about 10 minutes or until frittata is almost set.
5 Sprinkle cheese over frittata; place under grill until frittata is set and top is browned lightly.

on the table in 35 minutes
serves 4 **per serving** 7.8g total fat (4.9g saturated fat); 815kJ (195 cal); 13.0g carbohydrate; 16.7g protein; 2.8g fibre
tips frittata can be served hot or at room temperature. You can freeze the yolks, in packages of two or four, for future use when baking or when making custard. You can use frozen peas instead of fresh peas, if you like.

Chicken tandoori pockets with raita

400g chicken tenderloins
1 tablespoon lime juice
⅓ cup (100g) tandoori paste
¼ cup (70g) low-fat yogurt
8 large flour tortillas
60g snow pea tendrils
raita
1 cup (280g) low-fat yogurt
1 lebanese cucumber (130g), halved, seeded, chopped finely
1 tablespoon finely chopped fresh mint

1 Combine chicken with juice, paste and yogurt in medium bowl.
2 Cook chicken, in batches, on heated oiled grill plate (or grill or barbecue) until cooked through. Stand 5 minutes; slice thickly.
3 Heat tortillas according to manufacturer's instructions.
4 Meanwhile, make raita.
5 Place equal amounts of each of the chicken, tendrils and raita on a quarter section of each tortilla; fold tortilla in half and then in half again to enclose filling and form triangle-shaped pockets.
raita combine ingredients in small bowl.

on the table in 20 minutes
makes 8 **per pocket** 8.4g total fat (1.3g saturated fat); 1137kJ (272 cal); 28.3g carbohydrate; 18.9g protein; 3.0g fibre

Peking duck rolls

½ chinese barbecued duck
2 green onions
12 x 17cm-square rice paper sheets
2 tablespoons hoisin sauce
1 tablespoon plum sauce
1 lebanese cucumber (130g), seeded, cut into batons

1 Remove skin and meat from duck. Discard bones; slice meat and skin thinly. Cut each onion crossways into three equal pieces; slice pieces thinly lengthways.
2 To assemble rolls, place 1 sheet of rice paper in medium bowl of warm water until just softened. Lift sheet from water carefully; place, with one point of the square sheet facing you, on board covered with tea towel. Spread 1 teaspoon of combined sauces vertically along centre of sheet; top with a little of the cucumber, a little of the green onion and a little of the duck meat. Fold top and bottom corners over filling then roll sheet from side to side to enclose filling. Repeat with remaining rice paper sheets, combined sauces, cucumber, onion and duck.

on the table in 20 minutes
makes 12 rolls **per roll** 6.5g total fat (1.9g saturated fat); 439kJ (105 cal); 5.9g carbohydrate; 5.4g protein; 0.7g fibre

Poached eggs and asparagus with dill sauce

20g butter
¼ teaspoon saffron threads
1 teaspoon dijon mustard
1 tablespoon plain flour
1 cup (250ml) vegetable stock
2 tablespoons finely chopped fresh dill
750g asparagus, trimmed
4 eggs

1 Melt butter with saffron in small saucepan over medium heat; stir in mustard. Add flour; cook, stirring, until mixture thickens and bubbles. Gradually add stock; stir until mixture boils and thickens. Stir in dill.
2 Meanwhile, boil, steam or microwave asparagus until just tender, drain; cover to keep warm.
3 Half-fill a large shallow frying pan with water; bring to a boil. Break eggs into cup then slide into pan, one at a time. When all eggs are in pan, allow water to return to a boil. Cover pan, turn off heat; stand 4 minutes or until a light film of egg white sets over yolks. Using egg slide, remove eggs, one at a time, and place on absorbent-paper-lined saucer to blot up poaching liquid.
4 Divide asparagus among serving plates; top with eggs, drizzle with dill sauce.

on the table in 25 minutes
serves 4 **per serving** 9.8g total fat (4.4g saturated fat); 640kJ (153 cal); 4.5g carbohydrate; 10.9g protein; 2.0g fibre

Steamed sweet chilli prawn dumplings

500g uncooked medium prawns
2 tablespoons sweet chilli sauce
2 green onions, sliced thinly
1 clove garlic, crushed
5cm piece fresh ginger (10g), grated
2 tablespoons coarsely chopped fresh coriander
½ x 10cm stick (10g) finely chopped fresh lemon grass
24 gow gee wrappers

1 Shell and devein prawns; chop finely.
2 Combine prawn, sauce, onion, garlic, ginger, coriander and lemon grass in medium bowl.
3 Place 1 heaped teaspoon of the prawn filling in centre of each gow gee wrapper; brush edges with water. Fold wrapper in half to enclose filling; pinch edges together to seal.
4 Place dumplings, in batches, in single layer in bamboo steamer. Cook, covered, over wok of simmering water about 5 minutes or until dumplings are cooked through.

on the table in 25 minutes
serves 6 **per serving** 1.0g total fat (0.2g saturated fat); 468kJ (112 cal); 14.0g carbohydrate; 10.9g protein; 1.2g fibre
tip wonton wrappers can be used as an alternative to gow gee wrappers.

Felafel burgers

2 x 300g cans chickpeas, rinsed, drained
1 medium brown onion (150g), chopped coarsely
2 cloves garlic, quartered
½ cup coarsely chopped fresh flat-leaf parsley
2 teaspoons ground coriander
1 teaspoon ground cumin
2 tablespoons plain flour
1 teaspoon bicarbonate of soda
1 egg, beaten lightly
1 long loaf turkish bread (430g)
1 large tomato (220g), sliced thinly
20g baby rocket leaves
yogurt and tahini sauce
¼ cup (70g) low-fat yogurt
2 tablespoons tahini
1 tablespoon lemon juice

1 Blend or process chickpeas, onion, garlic, parsley, coriander, cumin, flour, soda and egg until almost smooth. Using hands, shape mixture into four felafel patties. Cook felafel on heated oiled flat plate, uncovered, about 10 minutes or until browned both sides.
2 Make yogurt and tahini sauce.
3 Cut bread into quarters; toast both sides on heated oiled grill plate.
4 Split each piece of bread in half horizontally; sandwich sauce, tomato, felafel and rocket between bread halves.
yogurt and tahini sauce combine ingredients in small bowl.

on the table in 25 minutes
serves 4 **per serving** 13.1g total fat (2.0g saturated fat); 2115kJ (506 cal); 69.1g carbohydrate; 22.1g protein; 10.4g fibre
tip when cooking felafel, use two spatulas to turn them carefully.

Spinach and cheese quesadillas

⅔ cup (130g) low-fat cottage cheese
100g spinach leaves, trimmed
1 medium avocado (230g), chopped finely
1 cup (200g) canned mexican-style beans, drained
125g can corn kernels, drained
2 medium tomatoes (380g), seeded, chopped finely
1 small red onion (100g), chopped finely
2 medium zucchini (240g), grated coarsely
16 small flour tortillas
1½ cups (150g) coarsely grated low-fat mozzarella cheese

1 Preheat grill.
2 Blend or process cottage cheese and spinach until smooth. Combine avocado, beans, corn, tomato, onion and zucchini in medium bowl.
3 Place eight tortillas on lightly oiled oven tray; divide spinach mixture among tortillas, leaving 2cm border around edge. Divide avocado mixture among tortillas; top each with one of the remaining tortillas.
4 Sprinkle mozzarella over quesadilla stacks; place under grill until cheese just melts and browns lightly.

on the table in 30 minutes
serves 8 **per serving** 11.3g total fat (3.8g saturated fat); 1170kJ (280 cal); 26.8g carbohydrate; 15.4g protein; 4.3g fibre
tip quesadillas are filled tortillas which are grilled or fried and served with fresh salsa. We used small flour tortillas measuring about 16cm in diameter; they are sometimes labelled "fajita tortillas" on the package.

salads

Vietnamese chicken salad

500g chicken breast fillets
1 large carrot (180g)
½ cup (125ml) rice wine vinegar
2 teaspoons salt
2 tablespoons caster sugar
1 medium white onion (150g), sliced thinly
1½ cups (120g) bean sprouts
2 cups (160g) finely shredded savoy cabbage
¼ cup firmly packed vietnamese mint leaves
½ cup firmly packed fresh coriander leaves
1 tablespoon crushed toasted peanuts
2 tablespoons fried shallots
vietnamese dressing
2 tablespoons fish sauce
¼ cup (60ml) water
2 tablespoons caster sugar
2 tablespoons lime juice
1 clove garlic, crushed

1 Place chicken in medium saucepan of boiling water; return to a boil.
Reduce heat, simmer, uncovered, 10 minutes or until cooked through.
Cool chicken in poaching liquid 10 minutes; discard liquid (or reserve for
another use). Shred chicken coarsely.
2 Meanwhile, cut carrot into matchstick-sized pieces. Combine carrot in
large bowl with vinegar, salt and sugar, cover; stand 5 minutes. Add onion,
cover; stand 5 minutes. Add sprouts, cover; stand 3 minutes.
Drain pickled vegetables; discard liquid.
3 Make vietnamese dressing.
4 Place pickled vegetables in large bowl with chicken, cabbage, herbs
and dressing; toss to combine. Sprinkle with nuts and shallots.
vietnamese dressing place ingredients in screw-top jar; shake well.

on the table in 35 minutes
serves 4 **per serving** 8.9g total fat (2.3g saturated fat); 1271kJ (304 cal);
24.3g carbohydrate; 31g protein; 5.1g fibre
tip fried shallots provide an extra crunchy finish to a salad, stir-fry or
curry. They can be purchased at all Asian grocery stores; once opened,
they will keep for months if stored in a tightly sealed glass jar.

Thai pork salad with kaffir lime dressing

600g pork fillets
2 tablespoons grated palm sugar
1 tablespoon finely grated lime rind
2 teaspoons peanut oil
350g watercress, trimmed
1 cup loosely packed thai basil leaves
½ cup loosely packed fresh coriander leaves
½ cup loosely packed fresh mint leaves
1½ cups (120g) bean sprouts
1 medium green capsicum (200g), sliced thinly
kaffir lime dressing
2 cloves garlic, crushed
3 shallots (75g), sliced thinly
1 fresh small red thai chilli, sliced thinly
3 fresh kaffir lime leaves, sliced thinly
¼ cup (60ml) lime juice
⅓ cup (80ml) fish sauce
2 teaspoons grated palm sugar

1 Cut pork fillets in half horizontally. Combine pork with sugar, rind and oil in large bowl.
2 Cook pork mixture, in batches, in heated oiled large frying pan, over medium heat, about 15 minutes or until just cooked through. Cover pork; stand 5 minutes, then slice thinly.
3 Make kaffir lime dressing.
4 Place pork in large bowl with remaining ingredients and dressing; toss gently to combine.
kaffir lime dressing place ingredients in screw-top jar; shake well.

on the table in 30 minutes
serves 4 **per serving** 6.4g total fat (1.6g saturated fat); 1104kJ (264 cal); 12.2g carbohydrate; 38.8g protein; 5.8g fibre

Caesar salad

4 slices white bread
4 slices prosciutto (40g)
4 baby cos lettuces
¼ cup (20g) finely grated parmesan cheese
dressing
¼ cup (70g) low-fat yogurt
¼ cup (75g) low-fat mayonnaise
2 cloves garlic, quartered
5 anchovy fillets, drained
½ teaspoon worcestershire sauce
½ teaspoon dijon mustard
1½ tablespoons lemon juice

1 Preheat oven to 180°C/160°C fan-forced.
2 Remove crusts from bread; cut bread into 1cm cubes. Place on oven tray; bake, uncovered, 5 minutes or until croutons are just toasted lightly.
3 Cook prosciutto, uncovered, in oiled frying pan until browned and crisp; chop coarsely.
4 Make dressing.
5 Combine croutons, prosciutto and dressing in large bowl with lettuce leaves and cheese; toss gently to combine.
dressing blend or process yogurt, mayonnaise, garlic, anchovy, sauce, mustard and juice until almost smooth.

on the table in 25 minutes
serves 8 **per serving** 4.7g total fat (1.1g saturated fat); 410kJ (98 cal); 9.1g carbohydrate; 4.5g protein; 0.9g fibre

Chicken and crunchy noodle salad

4 chicken breast fillets (680g)
500g baby buk choy, shredded coarsely
250g cherry tomatoes, halved
50g fresh shiitake mushrooms, sliced thinly
¼ cup firmly packed fresh coriander leaves
1 cup (80g) bean sprouts
3 green onions, sliced thinly
100g crispy fried noodles
dressing
⅓ cup (80ml) light soy sauce
1 teaspoon sesame oil
2 tablespoons dry sherry

1 Cook chicken, in batches, on heated oiled grill plate (or grill or barbecue) until browned both sides and cooked through. Stand 5 minutes; slice thinly.
2 Make dressing.
3 Place chicken in large bowl with remaining ingredients and dressing in large bowl; toss gently to combine.
dressing place ingredients in screw-top jar; shake well.

on the table in 20 minutes
serves 4 **per serving** 7.6g total fat (2.1g saturated fat); 1246kJ (298 cal); 9.0g carbohydrate; 43.2g protein; 4.4g fibre

Tuna and white bean salad

2 x 300g cans white beans, drained, rinsed
425g can tuna in springwater, drained, flaked
1 medium red onion (170g), sliced thinly
½ cup coarsely chopped fresh flat-leaf parsley
1 tablespoon coarsely chopped fresh oregano
250g cherry tomatoes, quartered
1 long loaf turkish bread
dressing
2 tablespoons olive oil
1 tablespoon white vinegar
2 teaspoons finely grated lemon rind
2 tablespoons lemon juice
2 cloves garlic, crushed

1 Make dressing.
2 Place beans and tuna in large bowl with onion, parsley, oregano, tomato and dressing; toss gently to combine.
3 Quarter bread crossways; slice pieces in half horizontally. Cut bread again, on the diagonal, to make 16 triangles; toast triangles, cut-side up.
4 Place one triangle, toasted-side up, on each serving plate; top with salad, then remaining triangles.
dressing place ingredients in screw-top jar; shake well.

on the table in 20 minutes
serves 8 **per serving** 6.7g total fat (1.2g saturated fat); 794kJ (190 cal); 16.6g carbohydrate; 14.2g protein; 3.0g fibre
tip many varieties of pre-cooked white beans are available canned, among them cannellini, butter and haricot beans; any of these are suitable for this salad.

Pan-fried tofu with vietnamese coleslaw salad

400g firm silken tofu
4 small carrots (280g)
2 cups (160g) finely shredded green cabbage
2 cups (160g) finely shredded red cabbage
2 small yellow capsicums (300g), sliced thinly
2 cups (160g) bean sprouts
8 green onions, sliced thinly
1 cup loosely packed fresh coriander leaves
lime and garlic dressing
1 cup (250ml) lime juice
2 cloves garlic, crushed

1 Place tofu, in single layer, on absorbent-paper-lined tray; cover tofu with more absorbent paper, stand 10 minutes.
2 Meanwhile, using vegetable peeler, slice carrots into ribbons. Place ribbons in medium bowl with cabbages, capsicum, sprouts, onion and coriander; toss gently to combine.
3 Cut tofu into slices; cook tofu in heated oiled small frying pan until browned both sides.
4 Make lime and garlic dressing, drizzle over salad; toss gently to combine. Serve salad with tofu.
lime and garlic dressing place ingredients in screw-top jar; shake well.

on the table in 30 minutes
serves 4 **per serving** 7.4g total fat (1.0g saturated fat); 836kJ (200 cal); 11.8g carbohydrate; 17.1g protein; 9.3g fibre

Beef with green papaya, chilli and coriander salad

600g piece beef rump steak
800g green papaya
2 medium tomatoes (300g), seeded, sliced thinly
3 cups (180g) finely shredded iceberg lettuce
2 lebanese cucumbers (260g), seeded, sliced thinly
dressing
⅓ cup (80ml) lime juice
2 tablespoons fish sauce
1 tablespoon brown sugar
2 cloves garlic, crushed
3 small green chillies, chopped finely
¼ cup coarsely chopped fresh coriander

1 Cook beef on heated oiled grill plate (or grill or barbecue), uncovered, until cooked as desired. Cover beef; stand 5 minutes, slice thinly.
2 Peel papaya. Quarter lengthways, discard seeds; grate papaya coarsely.
3 Make dressing.
4 Place beef and papaya in large bowl with tomato, lettuce, cucumber and dressing; toss gently to combine.
dressing place ingredients in screw-top jar; shake well.

on the table in 35 minutes
serves 4 **per serving** 10.4g total fat (4.5g saturated fat); 1300kJ (311 cal); 15.3g carbohydrate; 36.2g protein; 5.3g fibre

Thai chicken salad

You will need to buy a large barbecued chicken weighing about 900g for this recipe.

350g yellow string beans, trimmed, halved
1 teaspoon finely grated lime rind
2 tablespoons lime juice
1 tablespoon grated palm sugar
1 clove garlic, crushed
1 tablespoon peanut oil
½ cup finely chopped fresh mint
2 teaspoons sweet chilli sauce
1 tablespoon fish sauce
3 cups (480g) shredded cooked chicken
1 cup coarsely chopped fresh coriander
250g cherry tomatoes, halved
1 fresh small red thai chilli, chopped finely

1 Boil, steam or microwave beans until almost tender. Rinse under cold water; drain.
2 Combine rind, juice, sugar, garlic, oil, mint and sauces in large bowl. Add beans, chicken, three-quarters of the coriander and tomato; toss gently to combine.
3 Top salad with remaining coriander and chilli just before serving.

on the table in 20 minutes
serves 4 **per serving** 12.0g total fat (2.9g saturated fat); 1078kJ (258 cal); 7.9g carbohydrate; 27.6g protein; 4.2g fibre

Soba and daikon salad

300g dried soba noodles
1 small daikon (400g), cut into matchsticks
4 green onions, sliced thinly
1 teaspoon sesame oil
100g enoki mushrooms
2 tablespoons thinly sliced pickled ginger
1 toasted seaweed sheet (yaki-nori), sliced thinly
mirin dressing
¼ cup (60ml) mirin
2 tablespoons kecap manis
1 tablespoon sake
1 clove garlic, crushed
1cm piece fresh ginger (5g), grated
1 teaspoon white sugar

1 Cook noodles in large saucepan of boiling water, uncovered, until just tender; drain. Rinse under cold water; drain.
2 Meanwhile, make mirin dressing.
3 Place noodles in large bowl with daikon, onion and half of the mirin dressing; toss gently to combine.
4 Heat oil in small frying pan; cook mushrooms, stirring, 2 minutes.
5 Divide salad among serving plates; top with combined mushrooms, ginger and seaweed. Drizzle with remaining dressing.
mirin dressing place ingredients in screw-top jar; shake well.

on the table in 35 minutes
serves 4 **per serving** 6.0g total fat (1.6g saturated fat); 694kJ (166 cal); 12.8g carbohydrate; 11.2g protein; 6.9g fibre

Japanese omelette salad

1 medium daikon (600g)
2 medium carrots (240g)
6 large red radishes (210g), sliced thinly
1½ cups (120g) finely shredded red cabbage
1½ cups (120g) bean sprouts
2 tablespoons pink pickled ginger, sliced thinly
6 green onions, sliced thinly
4 eggs, beaten lightly
1 tablespoon soy sauce
½ sheet toasted seaweed (yaki-nori), sliced thinly
wasabi dressing
1 tablespoon pink pickled ginger juice
2 tablespoons soy sauce
1 tablespoon mirin
1 teaspoon wasabi paste

1 Using vegetable peeler, slice daikon and carrots into ribbons. Place ribbons in large bowl with radish, cabbage, sprouts, ginger and three-quarters of the onion.
2 Combine egg, sauce and seaweed in small jug. Pour half of the egg mixture in large heated oiled frying pan; cook, uncovered, until just set. Slide omelette onto plate; roll into cigar shape. Slice omelette roll into thin rings. Repeat with remaining egg mixture.
3 Make wasabi dressing.
4 Add dressing to salad; toss gently to combine. Divide salad among serving bowls; top with omelette rings and remaining onion.
wasabi dressing place ingredients in screw-top jar; shake well.

on the table in 25 minutes
serves 4 **per serving** 10.4g carbohydrate; 6.2g total fat (1.7g saturated fat); 610kj (146 cal); 11.7g protein

Asian crispy noodle salad

½ medium wombok (500g), shredded finely
227g can water chestnuts, drained, sliced thinly
150g snow peas, trimmed, sliced thinly
1 large red capsicum (350g), sliced thinly
100g crispy fried noodles
⅓ cup (50g) toasted unsalted cashews, chopped coarsely
1 cup loosely packed fresh coriander leaves
sesame soy dressing
1 teaspoon sesame oil
¼ cup (60ml) soy sauce
1 tablespoon sweet chilli sauce
2 tablespoons lime juice

1 Place wombok, water chestnuts, snow peas, capsicum and fried noodles in medium bowl.
2 Make sesame soy dressing.
3 Divide salad among serving bowls; sprinkle with nuts and coriander, drizzle with dressing.
sesame soy dressing place ingredients in screw-top jar; shake well.

on the table in 15 minutes
serves 4 **per serving** 10.8g fat (2.2g saturated fat); 869kJ (208 cal); 19.1g carbohydrate; 8.3g protein; 6.4g fibre

Roasted egg tomatoes with barley salad

1 cup (200g) pearl barley
8 medium egg tomatoes (600g), cut into thick wedges
4 small green capsicum (600g), chopped finely
2 small red onions (200g), chopped finely
2 cups coarsely chopped fresh flat-leaf parsley
lemon and dill dressing
⅔ cup (160ml) lemon juice
⅓ cup finely chopped fresh dill
1 tablespoon olive oil
2 cloves garlic, crushed

1 Preheat oven to 240°C/220°C fan-forced.
2 Cook barley in small saucepan of boiling water, uncovered, about 20 minutes or until just tender; drain. Rinse under cold water; drain.
3 Meanwhile, place tomato, cut-side up, on oiled oven tray. Roast, uncovered, about 15 minutes or until just softened.
4 Make lemon and dill dressing.
5 Place barley and half of the tomato in medium bowl with capsicum, onion, parsley and dressing; toss gently to combine. Served topped with remaining tomato.
lemon and dill dressing place ingredients in screw-top jar; shake well.

on the table in 35 minutes
serves 4 **per serving** 6.4g total fat (0.9g saturated fat); 1191kJ (285 cal); 44.4g carbohydrate; 10.7g protein; 13.4 fibre

White bean salad

50g mesclun
½ cup (100g) canned white beans, rinsed, drained
2 tablespoons coarsely chopped fresh tarragon
2 tablespoons coarsely chopped fresh flat-leaf parsley
1 small carrot (70g), cut into matchsticks
½ lebanese cucumber (65g), cut into matchsticks
2 red radishes (70g), trimmed, cut into matchsticks
2 tablespoons apple juice
1 tablespoon apple cider vinegar
1 tablespoon toasted sunflower seeds
1 tablespoon toasted pepitas

1 Place mesclun, beans, herbs, carrot, cucumber, radish, juice and vinegar in medium bowl; toss gently to combine.
2 Serve salad topped with seeds.

on the table in 15 minutes
serves 1 **per serving** 12.3g total fat (0.5g saturated fat); 1145kJ (274 cal); 21g carbohydrate; 10.1g protein; 12.5g fibre
tip many varieties of pre-cooked white beans are available canned, among them cannellini, butter and haricot beans; any of these are suitable for this salad.

Panzanella

1 litre (4 cups) water
250g stale sourdough bread, cut into 2cm slices
2 large tomatoes (440g), chopped coarsely
1 small red onion (100g), sliced thinly
2 lebanese cucumbers (260g), chopped coarsely
1 cup firmly packed fresh basil leaves
2 tablespoons olive oil
2 tablespoons red wine vinegar
1 clove garlic, crushed

1 Place the water in large shallow bowl; briefly dip bread slices into water. Pat dry with absorbent paper; tear bread into large chunks.
2 Place bread in large bowl with remaining ingredients; toss gently to combine.

on the table in 20 minutes
serves 4 **per serving** 11g total fat (1.5g saturated fat); 1104kJ (264 cal); 33.2g carbohydrate; 7.5g protein; 6g fibre

Potato and bean salad with lemon yogurt dressing

2 small potatoes (240g), unpeeled, cut into wedges
150g green beans, trimmed, cut into 3cm lengths
230g baby rocket leaves
½ small red onion (50g), sliced thinly
lemon yogurt dressing
⅓ cup (95g) low-fat yogurt
1 teaspoon finely grated lemon rind
1 tablespoon fresh lemon juice
1 tablespoon finely chopped fresh flat-leaf parsley

1 Boil, steam or microwave potato and beans, separately, until tender; drain. Rinse beans under cold water; drain.
2 Place potato and beans in medium bowl with rocket and onion; toss gently to combine.
3 Make lemon yogurt dressing; drizzle over salad to serve.
lemon yogurt dressing combine ingredients in small bowl.

on the table in 30 minutes
serves 1 **per serving** 6.6g total fat (1g saturated fat); 1308kJ (313 cal); 43.9g carbohydrate; 15.2g protein; 10.3g fibre

Warm rice and chickpea salad

1 cup (200g) doongara rice
1¾ cups (430ml) water
300g can chickpeas, rinsed, drained
¼ cup (40g) sultanas
¼ cup (35g) dried apricots, chopped finely
2 green onions, sliced thinly
2 tablespoons toasted pine nuts
balsamic orange dressing
1 teaspoon finely grated orange rind
⅓ cup (80ml) orange juice
1 tablespoon balsamic vinegar
1 clove garlic, crushed
1cm piece fresh ginger (5g), grated

1 Combine rice and the water in medium heavy-based saucepan; bring to a boil. Reduce heat; simmer, covered, about 8 minutes or until rice is tender. Remove from heat; stand, covered, 10 minutes. Fluff rice with fork.
2 Meanwhile, make balsamic orange dressing.
3 Place rice in large bowl with remaining ingredients and dressing; toss gently to combine.
balsamic orange dressing place ingredients in screw-top jar; shake well.

on the table in 35 minutes
serves 6 **per serving** 4.3g total fat (0.3g saturated fat); 953kJ (228 cal); 39.8g carbohydrate; 5.5g protein; 3.1g fibre
tip doongara rice has a lower glycaemic index than most other types of rice, and can be found at your local supermarket.

Pickled green papaya salad

1 cup (250ml) water
½ cup (125ml) rice vinegar
½ cup (110g) white sugar
1 teaspoon salt
1 fresh long red chilli, halved lengthways
1 small green papaya (650g)
150g sugar snap peas
100g bean thread noodles
1 small red onion (100g), sliced thinly
½ small pineapple (450g), quartered, sliced thinly
1 cup firmly packed fresh mint leaves
1 fresh long red chilli, sliced thinly
palm sugar dressing
¼ cup (60ml) lime juice
2 tablespoons grated palm sugar

1 Combine the water, vinegar, sugar, salt and halved chilli in small saucepan; bring to a boil. Reduce heat, simmer, uncovered, 5 minutes. Strain into small jug; discard solids. Cool 10 minutes.
2 Meanwhile, peel papaya. Quarter lengthways, discard seeds. Grate papaya coarsely; place in medium bowl with vinegar mixture. Cover; stand until required.
3 Boil, steam or microwave peas until just tender; drain. Place noodles in medium heatproof bowl, cover with boiling water; stand until just tender, drain. Rinse under cold water; drain. Using kitchen scissors, cut noodles into random lengths.
4 Make palm sugar dressing.
5 Place drained papaya, peas and noodles in medium bowl with onion, pineapple, mint and dressing; toss gently to combine.
6 Divide salad among serving bowls; top with sliced chilli.
palm sugar dressing place ingredients in screw-top jar; shake well.

on the table in 35 minutes
serves 4 **per serving** 0.4g total fat (0.0g saturated fat); 577kJ (138 cal); 29g carbohydrate; 3.1g protein; 6.4g fibre
tip green (unripe) papayas are readily available in various sizes at many Asian food shops and markets. Select one that is very hard and slightly shiny, which indicates it's fresh but not too unripe to grate or chop.

Mixed bean salad

½ x 300g can four-bean mix, rinsed, drained
1 trimmed celery stalk (100g), chopped finely
½ medium yellow capsicum (100g), chopped finely
¼ cup (30g) seeded black olives, chopped coarsely
¼ cup loosely packed fresh flat-leaf parsley leaves
½ small red onion (50g), sliced thinly
20g baby rocket leaves
dressing
1 clove garlic, crushed
2 teaspoons olive oil
2 teaspoons fresh lemon juice

1 Make dressing.
2 Place beans in medium bowl with remaining ingredients and dressing; toss gently to combine.
dressing place ingredients in screw-top jar; shake well.

on the table in 15 minutes
serves 1 **per serving** 10.3g total fat (1.5g saturated fat); 995kJ (238 cal); 27.6g carbohydrate; 9.3g protein; 10.5g fibre

Green vegetable salad with american mustard dressing

200g green beans, trimmed
200g snow peas, trimmed
200g sugar snap peas, trimmed
1 cup loosely packed fresh flat-leaf parsley leaves
½ cups loosely packed fresh chervil leaves
100g baby rocket leaves
⅓ cup (50g) dried currants
american mustard dressing
2 tablespoons american mustard
2 tablespoons lemon juice
2 tablespoons olive oil

1 Boil, steam or microwave beans and peas, separately, until just tender; drain. Rinse beans and peas under cold water; drain.
2 Place beans and peas in medium bowl with herbs, rocket and currants; toss gently to combine.
3 Make american mustard dressing; drizzle over salad.
american mustard dressing place ingredients in screw-top jar; shake well.

on the table in 35 minutes
serves 4 **per serving** 9.9g total fat (1.3g saturated fat); 715kJ (171 cal); 15g carbohydrate; 5.7g protein; 5.6g fibre

Salade niçoise

200g green beans, trimmed, chopped coarsely
250g cherry tomatoes, halved
½ cup (80g) seeded black olives
2 lebanese cucumbers (260g), sliced thickly
1 medium red onion (170g), sliced thinly
150g mesclun
6 hard-boiled eggs, quartered
425g can tuna in springwater, drained
light vinaigrette
1 teaspoon olive oil
¼ cup (60ml) lemon juice
1 clove garlic, crushed
2 teaspoons dijon mustard

1 Boil, steam or microwave beans until just tender; drain. Rinse under cold water; drain.
2 Make light vinaigrette.
3 Place beans in large bowl with tomato, olives, cucumber, onion, mesclun, egg and vinaigrette; toss gently to combine.
4 Divide salad among serving plates; flake fish over salad in large chunks.
light vinaigrette place ingredients in screw-top jar; shake well.

on the table in 30 minutes
serves 4 **per serving** 12.4g total fat (3.6g saturated fat); 1262kJ (302 cal); 11.9g carbohydrate; 33.1g protein; 4.9g fibre

Pearl barley salad

1 cup (400g) pearl barley
500g asparagus, trimmed, cut into 4cm lengths
500g cherry tomatoes, halved
2 lebanese cucumber (260g), sliced thinly
3 cups (180g) finely shredded iceberg lettuce
⅔ cup coarsely chopped fresh basil
⅔ cup (160ml) lemon juice

1 Cook barley in small saucepan of boiling water, uncovered, about
25 minutes or until tender; drain. Cool 5 minutes.
2 Meanwhile, boil, steam or microwave asparagus until just tender; drain.
3 Place barley and asparagus in medium bowl with remaining ingredients;
toss gently to combine.

on the table in 35 minutes
serves 4 **per serving** 2.9g total fat (0.4g saturated fat); 1513kJ (362 cal);
68.4g carbohydrate; 13.5g protein; 17g fibre

Mexican bean salad with tortilla chips

4 medium tomatoes (600g), seeded, chopped coarsely
420g can four-bean mix, rinsed, drained
300g can kidney beans, rinsed, drained
½ cup coarsely chopped fresh coriander
¼ cup (60ml) lime juice
1 small red onion (100g), chopped finely
2 fresh long red chillies, chopped finely
4 small flour tortillas, cut into wedges
1 small avocado (200g)
2 tablespoons light sour cream

1 Preheat oven to 200°C/180°C fan-forced.
2 Combine tomato, beans, ⅓ cup of the coriander, 1 tablespoon of the juice, half of the onion and half of the chilli in medium bowl.
3 Place tortilla wedges, in single layer, on oven tray; toast 5 minutes or until crisp.
4 To make guacamole, mash avocado in small bowl; stir in remaining coriander, juice, onion and chilli.
5 Divide tortilla chips among plates; top with bean mixture, guacamole and sour cream.

on the table in 25 minutes
serves 4 **per serving** 14g total fat (3.7g saturated fat); 1522kJ (364 cal); 44.9g carbohydrate; 14.1g protein; 10.9g fibre

Grilled asparagus with warm tomato dressing

4 medium tomatoes (600g), chopped finely
2 cloves garlic, crushed
⅔ cup (180ml) lemon juice
⅓ cup finely chopped fresh basil
⅓ cup finely chopped fresh flat-leaf parsley
500g asparagus, trimmed
100g curly endive, torn
100g rocket

1 Place tomato, garlic and juice in small saucepan; bring to a boil. Reduce heat, simmer, uncovered, 2 minutes. Remove from heat; stir in herbs.
2 Meanwhile, cook asparagus on heated oiled grill plate (or grill or barbecue) until just tender.
3 Place endive and rocket on serving plates; top with asparagus and tomato dressing.

on the table in 35 minutes
serves 4 **per serving** 0.7g total fat (0.0g saturated fat); 272kJ (65 cal); 6.7g carbohydrate; 6.3g protein; 6.5g fibre

Soba salad with seaweed, ginger and vegetables

20g wakame
100g dried soba noodles
4 lebanese cucumbers (520g), seeded, cut into matchsticks
4 small carrots (280g), cut into matchsticks
⅓ cup (50g) toasted sesame seeds
4 green onions, sliced thinly
4cm piece fresh ginger (20g), grated
1 tablespoon sesame oil
⅔ cup (180ml) lime juice
1 tablespoon tamari

1 Place wakame in medium bowl, cover with cold water; stand about 10 minutes or until wakame softens, drain. Discard any hard stems; chop coarsely.
2 Meanwhile, cook noodles in medium saucepan of boiling water, uncovered, until just tender; drain. Rinse under cold water; drain. Chop noodles coarsely.
3 Place wakame and noodles in medium bowl with remaining ingredients; toss gently to combine.

on the table in 30 minutes
serves 4 **per serving** 12.2g total fat (1.6g saturated fat); 1053kJ (252 cal); 23.7g carbohydrate; 8.2g protein; 7.9g fibre
tips wakame, a bright green seaweed usually sold in dried form, is used in soups, salads and seasonings. Dried wakame must be softened by soaking for about 10 minutes, and any hard stems are then discarded. It is available from most Asian food stores. Soba is a Japanese noodle, similar in appearance to spaghetti, made from buckwheat.

Smoked chicken salad

400g smoked chicken breast
200g baby spinach leaves
1 medium yellow capsicum (200g), sliced thinly
1 medium red onion (170g), sliced thinly
1 cup firmly packed fresh purple basil leaves
dressing
2 teaspoons finely grated lime rind
¼ cup (60ml) lime juice
2 tablespoons coarsely chopped fresh coriander
2 fresh small red thai chillies, chopped finely
2 teaspoons peanut oil
1 teaspoon white sugar

1 Remove and discard any skin from chicken; slice chicken thinly.
2 Make dressing.
3 Place chicken in large bowl with spinach, capsicum, onion, basil and dressing; toss gently to combine.
dressing place ingredients in screw-top jar; shake well.

on the table in 15 minutes
serves 8 **per serving** 4.8g total fat (1.2g saturated fat); 464kJ (111 cal); 2.8g carbohydrate; 13.6g protein; 1.2g fibre
tips purple basil, sometimes called opal basil, is more aromatic than green basil. Smoked chicken has already been cooked during the curing process, making this a simple salad to put together at short notice. You can keep smoked chicken in your freezer; just thaw before slicing.

vegies+
grains

Nasi goreng

You will need to cook about 2 cups of jasmine rice the day before you want to make this — or any fried rice recipe. Spread the rice out in a thin layer on a tray, cover and refrigerate overnight.

1 small brown onion (80g), chopped coarsely
2 cloves garlic, quartered
5cm piece fresh ginger (25g), chopped
2 fresh long red chillies, chopped coarsely
1 tablespoon peanut oil
4 eggs, beaten lightly
150g oyster mushrooms, chopped coarsely
1 medium green capsicum (200g), chopped coarsely
1 medium red capsicum (200g), chopped coarsely
200g fresh baby corn, chopped coarsely
4 cups cooked jasmine rice
1 cup (80g) bean sprouts
3 green onions, sliced thinly
2 tablespoons soy sauce
1 tablespoon kecap manis

1 Blend or process brown onion, garlic, ginger and chilli until almost smooth.
2 Heat 1 teaspoon of the oil in wok; add half of the egg, swirl wok to make thin omelette. Cook, uncovered, until egg is just set. Remove from wok; cut into thick strips. Repeat process with another 1 teaspoon of the oil and remaining egg.
3 Heat remaining oil in wok; stir-fry onion mixture until fragrant. Add mushrooms, capsicums and corn; stir-fry until tender.
4 Add rice, sprouts, green onion and sauces; stir-fry until heated through.
5 Serve nasi goreng topped with omelette strips.

on the table in 35 minutes
serves 4 **per serving** 11.2g total fat (2.5g saturated fat); 1843kJ (441 cal); 66.8g carbohydrate; 17.6g protein; 7.2g fibre

Stir-fried asian greens with mixed mushrooms

2 teaspoons sesame oil
2 teaspoons vegetable oil
2 cloves garlic, crushed
3 x 10cm sticks (60g) finely chopped fresh lemon grass
8cm piece fresh ginger (40g), grated
600g oyster mushrooms, chopped coarsely
600g button mushrooms, chopped coarsely
600g baby buk choy, chopped coarsely
1 small wombok (700g), chopped coarsely

1 Heat oils in wok; stir-fry garlic, lemon grass, ginger and mushrooms until browned lightly. Add buk choy and wombok; stir-fry until greens are just wilted.
2 Serve stir-fry with lime wedges, if desired.

on the table in 20 minutes
serves 4 **per serving** 5.7g total fat (0.6g saturated fat); 656kJ (157 cal); 5.4g carbohydrate; 13.9g protein; 15.3g fibre

Eggplant with salsa fresca

12 baby eggplants (720g), halved lengthways
salsa fresca
2 small green capsicum (300g), chopped finely
2 small yellow capsicum (300g), chopped finely
4 small tomatoes (360g), seeded, chopped finely
⅔ cup finely shredded fresh basil
⅔ cup (160ml) lemon juice

1 Cook eggplant on heated lightly oiled grill plate (or grill or barbecue) until tender.
2 Make salsa fresca.
2 Serve grilled eggplant topped with salsa fresca.
salsa fresca combine ingredients in small bowl.

on the table in 35 minutes
serves 4 **per serving** 0.8g total fat (0.0g saturated fat); 288kJ (69 cal); 9.6g carbohydrate; 4.6g protein; 5.9g fibre

Pasta primavera

375g penne pasta
200g baby carrots, quartered lengthways
350g asparagus, trimmed, cut into 4cm lengths
150g snow peas, trimmed, halved
1 cup (120g) frozen peas
4 green onions, sliced thinly
2 medium egg tomatoes (150g), seeded, chopped finely
lemon thyme and mustard dressing
1 tablespoon dijon mustard
1 tablespoon white wine vinegar
1 tablespoon lemon juice
2 tablespoons water
2 tablespoons coarsely chopped fresh lemon thyme
1 tablespoon olive oil

1 Cook pasta in large saucepan of boiling water, uncovered, until just tender; drain. Rinse under cold water; drain.
2 Meanwhile, boil, steam or microwave carrot, asparagus and peas, separately, until tender; drain. Rinse under cold water; drain.
3 Make lemon thyme and mustard dressing.
4 Place pasta and vegetables in large bowl with onion, tomato and dressing; toss gently.
lemon thyme and mustard dressing place ingredients in screw-top jar; shake well.

on the table in 35 minutes
serves 4 **per serving** 6.1g total fat (0.8g saturated fat); 1747kJ (418 cal); 73.1g carbohydrate; 16.5g protein; 9g fibre

Singapore noodles

250g rice vermicelli noodles
4 eggs, beaten lightly
2 teaspoons vegetable oil
1 medium brown onion (150g), chopped coarsely
2 cloves garlic, crushed
2cm piece fresh ginger (10g), grated
150g baby buk choy, chopped coarsely
200g snow peas, halved
1 small red capsicum (150g), sliced thickly
2 tablespoons soy sauce
2 tablespoons oyster sauce
2 tablespoons sweet chilli sauce
1 cup loosely packed fresh coriander leaves
3 cups (240g) bean sprouts

1 Place noodles in large heatproof bowl, cover with boiling water, stand until just tender; drain. Using scissors, cut noodles into 10cm lengths.
2 Heat lightly oiled wok; add half of the egg, swirl wok to make thin omelette. Cook, uncovered, until egg is just set. Remove from wok; roll into cigar shape, cut into thin slices. Repeat with remaining egg.
3 Heat oil in wok; stir-fry onion until soft. Add garlic and ginger; cook, stirring, 1 minute. Add buk choy, snow peas, capsicum and sauces; cook, stirring, until vegetables are just tender.
4 Add noodles and egg strips to wok with coriander and sprouts; toss gently to combine.

on the table in 30 minutes
serves 4 **per serving** 8.3g total fat (2.0g saturated fat); 1463kJ (350 cal); 51.6g carbohydrate; 12.5g protein; 7.6g fibre

Artichoke risotto

2 teaspoons olive oil
1 medium brown onion (150g), chopped finely
3 cloves garlic, crushed
6 green onions, sliced thinly
2 cups (400g) doongara rice
¾ cup (180ml) dry white wine
1½ cups (375ml) chicken stock
3 cups (750ml) water
400g can artichoke hearts, drained, sliced thinly
½ cup (40g) finely grated parmesan cheese

1 Heat oil in large saucepan; cook brown onion, garlic and half of the green onion, stirring, until brown onion softens.
2 Add rice, wine, stock and the water; bring to a boil. Reduce heat, simmer, covered, 15 minutes, stirring occasionally.
3 Stir in artichokes, cheese and remaining green onion; cook, stirring, about 5 minutes or until artichokes are heated through.

on the table in 35 minutes
serves 6 **per serving** 4.5g total fat (1.8g saturated fat); 1367kJ (327 cal); 55.7g carbohydrate; 9.2g protein; 2.6g fibre
tip while the short-grained arborio is traditionally used in a risotto, we chose to use the long-grained doongara rice here because it has both a lower GI rating and is more amenable to being cooked with the liquids added all at once.

Vegetable stir-fry

2 teaspoons sesame oil
400g fresh shiitake mushrooms, sliced thickly
4 medium carrot (480g), sliced thinly
⅔ cup (180ml) water
400g broccoli, sliced thinly
300g snow peas, trimmed, sliced thickly
⅓ cup (80ml) tamari
4 green onions, sliced thinly

1 Heat oil in wok; stir-fry mushroom and carrot 2 minutes. Add the water; stir-fry 5 minutes or until carrot just softens. Add broccoli and snow peas; stir-fry until broccoli is just tender. Stir in tamari.
2 Serve stir-fry topped with onion.

on the table in 25 minutes
serves 4 **per serving** 5.4g total fat (0.8g saturated fat); 778kJ (186 cal); 23.7g carbohydrate; 10.8g protein; 11.7g fibre

Roasted vegetable stacks

4 baby fennel bulbs (520g)
4 medium egg tomatoes (300g), halved lengthways
2 small red capsicums (300g), sliced thickly
2 medium zucchini (240g), sliced thickly lengthways
4 baby eggplants (240g), sliced thickly
cooking-oil spray
⅓ cup finely chopped fresh flat-leaf parsley
⅓ cup (80ml) lemon juice
1 tablespoon olive oil

1 Preheat oven to 200°C/180°C fan-forced.
2 Reserve fennel tips from fennel; slice fennel thinly.
3 Place vegetables on oiled oven tray; spray with oil. Roast, uncovered, about 20 minutes or until vegetables soften. Stir in half of the parsley.
4 Stack vegetables on serving plates; drizzle with combined juice and oil, sprinkle with remaining parsley and coarsely chopped reserved fennel tips.

on the table in 35 minutes
serves 4 **per serving** 7.2g total fat (0.8g saturated fat); 514kJ (123 cal); 9.7g carbohydrate; 4.1g protein; 6.5g fibre

Lemon-fetta couscous with steamed vegetables

You will need about half a butternut pumpkin for this recipe.

600g butternut pumpkin, chopped coarsely
2 small green zucchini (180g), chopped coarsely
2 small yellow zucchini (180g), chopped coarsely
300g spinach, trimmed, chopped coarsely
2 cups (500ml) vegetable stock
2 cups (400g) couscous
¼ cup (60ml) lemon juice
⅓ cup coarsely chopped fresh basil
200g low-fat fetta cheese, chopped coarsely
¼ cup (50g) finely chopped preserved lemon rind
6 green onions, sliced thinly

1 Boil, steam or microwave pumpkin, green and yellow zucchini and spinach, separately, until tender; drain.
2 Bring stock to a boil in large saucepan. Add couscous, remove from heat, cover; stand about 5 minutes or until liquid is absorbed, fluffing with fork occasionally.
3 Place couscous and vegetables in large bowl with remaining ingredients; toss gently to combine.

on the table in 30 minutes
serves 4 **per serving** 9.3g total fat (5.4g saturated fat); 2445kJ (585 cal); 88.7g carbohydrate; 32.2g protein; 6.0g fibre
tip preserved lemons, a North African specialty, are quartered and preserved in salt and lemon juice. To use, remove and discard pulp, squeeze juice from rind, rinse rind well then use. Sold in jars or in bulk by delicatessens; once opened, store preserved lemon in the refrigerator.

Vegetarian sukiyaki

440g fresh udon noodles
8 fresh shiitake mushrooms
4 green onions, cut into 3cm lengths
100g baby spinach leaves
230g can bamboo shoots, drained
½ small wombok (350g), chopped coarsely
100g enoki mushrooms, trimmed
1 small leek (200g), chopped coarsely
2 medium carrots (240g), sliced thickly
350g firm tofu, diced into 2cm pieces
4 eggs
broth
1 cup (250ml) soy sauce
½ cup (125ml) cooking sake
½ cup (125ml) mirin
1 cup (250ml) water
½ cup (110g) white sugar

1 Rinse noodles under hot water; drain. Cut into random lengths. Remove and discard shiitake stems; cut a cross in the top of caps.
2 Place ingredients for broth in medium saucepan; cook over medium heat, stirring, until sugar dissolves.
3 Arrange all ingredients, except eggs, on platters or in bowls. Place broth in medium bowl. Break eggs into individual bowls; beat lightly.
4 Pour broth into sukiyaki (or electric frying pan) pan. Heat pan on portable gas cooker at the table; cook a quarter of the noodles and a quarter of the remaining ingredients in broth, uncovered, until just tender. Dip cooked ingredients into egg before eating. Repeat process until all the remaining noodles and ingredients are cooked.

on the table in 30 minutes
serves 4 **per serving** 11.9g total fat (2.5g saturated fat); 2232kJ (534 cal); 65.8g carbohydrate; 29g protein; 9.4g fibre
tip a traditional sukiyaki pan is available from Japanese food or homeware shops – an electric frying pan can also be used. Only a quarter of the sukiyaki is cooked at a time, and individual portions are eaten, in batches, by diners who dip the hot food into a lightly beaten raw egg (which cooks on contact). Customarily, any remaining broth and egg are mixed together in each diner's bowl then served over steamed rice at the end of the meal.

Stir-fried tofu with vegetables and lemon grass

2 teaspoons sesame oil
400g firm tofu, cut into 1cm pieces
4 small red capsicums (600g), sliced thinly
1.2kg baby buk choy, chopped coarsely
2 x 10cm sticks (40g) finely chopped fresh lemon grass
2 cloves garlic, crushed
1 cup loosely packed fresh coriander leaves

1 Heat oil in wok; stir-fry tofu, capsicum, buk choy, lemon grass and garlic until vegetables are just tender. Stir in coriander.
2 Serve stir-fry with lemon wedges, if desired.

on the table in 20 minutes
serves 4 **per serving** 12.4g total fat (1.7g saturated fat); 924kJ (221 cal); 9.7g carbohydrate; 17.7g protein; 8.2g fibre

seafood

Poached flathead with herb salad

3 litres (12 cups) water
4 cloves garlic, crushed
20cm piece fresh ginger (100g), sliced
8 flathead fillets (880g)
2 limes, cut into wedges
herb salad
1 cup loosely packed fresh mint leaves
1 cup loosely packed fresh coriander leaves
1 cup loosely packed fresh basil leaves, torn
2 small red onions (200g), sliced thinly
4 lebanese cucumbers (520g), seeded, sliced thinly
⅓ cup (80ml) lime juice
4cm piece fresh ginger (20g), grated

1 Place the water, garlic and ginger in medium frying pan; bring to a boil. Add fish, reduce heat; simmer, uncovered, about 5 minutes or until fish is cooked as desired. Remove fish with slotted spoon; discard liquid.
2 Make herb salad.
3 Serve fish with salad and lime wedges.
herb salad place ingredients in medium bowl; toss gently to combine.

on the table in 35 minutes
serves 4 **per serving** 3g total fat (1.0g saturated fat); 1124kJ (269 cal); 8.3g carbohydrate; 49.6g protein; 6.6g fibre
tip we used flathead for this recipe, but you can use any firm white-fleshed fish fillets.

Japanese-style tuna with red-maple radish

The combination of daikon and chilli treated in this way is commonly known in Japan as "red-maple radish", and can be used as an accompaniment to any Japanese dish using raw fish.

600g piece sashimi tuna
⅓ cup (80ml) rice vinegar
½ small daikon (200g), peeled
4 dried long red chillies, chopped finely
2 tablespoons mirin
1 teaspoon sesame oil
1 teaspoon black sesame seeds
1 sheet toasted seaweed (yaki-nori), shredded finely

1 Slice tuna as thinly as possible; place, in single layer, on large platter, drizzle with vinegar. Cover; refrigerate until required.
2 Grate daikon finely. Place daikon and chilli in fine sieve set over small bowl; stir with small wooden spoon to combine then press with back of spoon to extract as much daikon liquid as possible.
3 Drain vinegar from tuna; divide tuna among serving plates. Drizzle with combined mirin and oil; sprinkle with seeds. Serve with red-maple radish and seaweed.

on the table in 25 minutes
serves 4 **per serving** 10.3g total fat (3.7g saturated fat); 1091kJ (261 cal); 1.7g carbohydrate; 38.3g protein; 1.2g fibre
tip tuna sold as sashimi has to meet stringent guidelines regarding its handling and treatment after leaving the water. Nevertheless, it is best to seek local advice from authorities before eating any raw seafood.

Citrus-ginger steamed bream

1 medium lemon (140g)
2 medium oranges (480g)
2 cloves garlic, crushed
2cm piece fresh ginger (10g), grated
4 x 250g whole bream, cleaned
2 cups (400g) jasmine rice
⅓ cup loosely packed fresh basil leaves, torn

1 Using vegetable peeler, peel rind carefully from lemon and one orange; cut rinds into thin strips. Squeeze juice of lemon and both oranges into large bowl. Stir in rind, garlic and ginger. Score fish both sides; add to bowl, coat in mixture.
2 Fold 80cm-long piece of foil in half crossways; place one fish onto foil, spoon a quarter of the citrus-ginger mixture onto fish. Fold foil over fish to tightly enclose. Repeat with remaining fish and citrus-ginger mixture.
3 Place fish parcels in large steamer fitted over large saucepan of boiling water; steam, covered, about 15 minutes or until cooked as desired.
4 Meanwhile, cook rice in large saucepan of boiling water, uncovered, until just tender; drain.
5 Divide rice among serving plates; top with fish, drizzle with cooking juices, sprinkle with basil.

on the table in 35 minutes
serves 4 **per serving** 13.4g total fat (4.6g saturated fat); 2959kJ (708 cal); 86.6g carbohydrate; 56.8g protein; 3.4g fibre
tips we used whole bream for this recipe, but any fairly small white-fleshed fish can be used. You need four 80cm-long sheets of foil to wrap the fish. Use a zester, if you have one, to remove orange and lemon rind.

Char-grilled scallops with citrus salsa

32 scallops (800g), roe removed
1 small pink grapefruit (350g), chopped finely
1 large orange (300g), chopped finely
1 lime, chopped finely
1 small mango (300g), chopped finely
¼ cup finely chopped fresh thai basil
¼ cup finely chopped fresh mint
citrus dressing
2 tablespoons mirin
1 tablespoon orange juice
1 tablespoon lemon juice
1 tablespoon olive oil
1 teaspoon finely grated lime rind

1 Cook scallops, in batches, on heated oiled grill plate (or grill or barbecue) until browned both sides and cooked as desired.
2 Meanwhile, make citrus dressing.
3 Place fruit and herbs in medium bowl with half of the dressing; toss gently to combine.
4 Serve scallops with salsa; drizzle with remaining dressing.
citrus dressing place ingredients in screw-top jar; shake well.

on the table in 25 minutes
serves 4 **per serving** 6.2g total fat (1.0g saturated fat); 836kJ (200 cal); 9.2g carbohydrate; 24.5g protein; 1.7g fibre

Calamari teppanyaki

1 ½ cups (300g) white medium-grain rice
3 cups (750ml) water
1kg calamari rings
1 tablespoon peanut oil
1 fresh small red thai chilli, chopped finely
1 teaspoon finely grated lemon rind
1 clove garlic, crushed
2 tablespoons drained pickled pink ginger, sliced thinly
6 green onions, sliced thickly
2 lebanese cucumbers (260g), seeded, chopped finely
3 fresh small red thai chillies, chopped finely, extra
lemon soy dipping sauce
¼ cup (60ml) rice vinegar
1 tablespoon white sugar
1 tablespoon japanese soy sauce
1 teaspoon finely grated lemon rind

1 Place rice and the water in medium heavy-based saucepan; bring to a
boil, covered, stirring occasionally. Reduce heat, simmer, covered tightly,
about 10 minutes or until rice is cooked as desired. Remove from heat;
stand, covered, 5 minutes.
2 Meanwhile, combine calamari with oil, chilli, rind and garlic in large
bowl. Cook calamari on heated oiled flat plate, uncovered, until tender.
3 Make lemon soy dipping sauce.
4 Divide rice and calamari among serving plates with ginger, onion,
cucumber and extra chilli; serve with bowls of dipping sauce.
lemon soy dipping sauce heat vinegar, sugar and sauce in small
saucepan, stirring, until sugar dissolves. Remove from heat; stir in rind.

on the table in 30 minutes
serves 4 **per serving** 8.0g total fat (1.9g saturated fat); 2228kJ (533 cal);
65.4g carbohydrate; 47.5g protein; 1.7g fibre
tip teppanyaki is the name given to a traditional Japanese cooking style
where the food is cooked rapidly on a searingly hot grill plate on or near
the table. Pink pickled ginger, also known as gari, can be found in most
Asian grocery stores.

Grilled snapper with spicy tomato sauce

2 tablespoons olive oil
3 cloves garlic, crushed
3 shallots (75g), chopped finely
425g can chopped tomatoes
1 tablespoon dry sherry
1 tablespoon soy sauce
1 teaspoon sambal oelek
2 teaspoons white sugar
4 x 200g snapper fillets
75g baby spinach leaves
2 teaspoons red wine vinegar

1 Heat half of the oil in small frying pan; cook garlic and shallots, stirring, about 1 minute or until shallots are soft. Stir in undrained tomatoes, sherry, sauce, sambal and sugar; bring to a boil. Reduce heat, simmer, uncovered, about 10 minutes or until liquid has reduced by half.
2 Cook fish, uncovered, in heated oiled large frying pan about 10 minutes or until cooked as desired.
3 Place spinach in medium bowl with combined vinegar and remaining oil; toss gently to combine. Serve fish with spinach salad and spicy sauce.

on the table in 30 minutes
serves 4 **per serving** 12.7g total fat (2.5g saturated fat); 1325kJ (317 cal); 42.5g protein; 2.3g fibre

Steamed mussels with saffron, chilli and coriander

¾ cup (180ml) dry white wine
¼ teaspoon saffron threads
1 tablespoon fish sauce
2 teaspoons finely grated lime rind
2kg medium black mussels
1 tablespoon peanut oil
5cm piece fresh ginger (25g), grated
2 cloves garlic, crushed
3 fresh small red thai chillies, sliced thinly
½ cup loosely packed fresh coriander leaves

1 Bring wine to a boil in small saucepan. Stir in saffron, sauce and rind; remove from heat. Stand 10 minutes.
2 Scrub mussels; remove beards.
3 Heat oil in large saucepan; cook ginger, garlic and chilli, stirring, until fragrant. Add wine mixture and mussels; bring to a boil. Reduce heat, simmer, covered, about 5 minutes or until mussels open (discard any that do not).
4 Spoon mussels and broth into serving bowls; sprinkle with coriander.

on the table in 35 minutes
serves 6 **per serving** 1.3g total fat (0.9g saturated fat); 451kJ (108 cal); 3.8g carbohydrate; 8.4g protein; 0.6g fibre

Stir-fried prawns with pineapple and chilli salad

1.5kg uncooked large king prawns
1 clove garlic, crushed
2cm piece fresh ginger (10g), grated
4 green onions, sliced thinly
1 tablespoon sesame oil
pineapple and chilli salad
1 small fresh pineapple (800g)
2 medium mangoes (860g)
¼ cup (30g) coarsely chopped toasted peanuts
1 fresh long red chilli, sliced thinly
2 green onions, sliced thinly
1 tablespoon finely chopped fresh vietnamese mint
¼ cup finely chopped fresh coriander
2 tablespoons lime juice
1 tablespoon fish sauce
2 teaspoons white sugar

1 Make pineapple and chilli salad.
2 Shell and devein prawns, leaving tails intact. Combine prawns with garlic, ginger and onion in large bowl.
3 Heat oil in wok; stir-fry prawn mixture until prawns are just changed in colour.
4 Divide salad among serving plates; top with prawns.
pineapple and chilli salad slice pineapple and mango thinly; cut slices into 5mm matchsticks. Place fruit in large bowl with nuts, chilli, onion and herbs. Place juice, sauce and sugar in screw-top jar; shake well. Add dressing to salad; toss gently to combine.

on the table in 35 minutes
serves 4 **per serving** 9.8g total fat (1.4g saturated fat); 1689kJ (404 cal); 31.6g carbohydrate; 43.7g protein; 5.7g fibre

Thai fish burgers with sour and sweet green salad

500g blue-eye fillets, chopped coarsely
1 tablespoon fish sauce
1 tablespoon kecap manis
1 clove garlic, quartered
1 fresh small red thai chilli, quartered
50g green beans, trimmed, chopped coarsely
¼ cup (15g) shredded coconut
¼ cup finely chopped fresh coriander
½ loaf turkish bread (215g)
⅓ cup (80ml) sweet chilli sauce
sour and sweet green salad
2 cups (120g) finely shredded iceberg lettuce
40g snow pea sprouts, chopped coarsely
1 telegraph cucumber (400g), seeded, sliced thinly
2 tablespoons lime juice
1 tablespoon fish sauce
1 tablespoon brown sugar

1 Blend or process fillets, sauce, kecap manis, garlic and chilli until smooth. Place in large bowl with beans, coconut and coriander; using hand, combine ingredients then shape mixture into four patties.
2 Cook patties on heated oiled flat plate, covered, about 15 minutes or until cooked through.
3 Meanwhile, make sour and sweet green salad.
4 Cut bread in half; split halves horizontally. Toast, cut-side up. Divide bread among serving plates; top with salad, patties and chilli sauce.
sour and sweet green salad place ingredients in medium bowl; toss gently to combine.

on the table in 35 minutes
serves 4 **per serving** 7.8g total fat (3.4g saturated fat); 1522kJ (364 cal); 36.5g carbohydrate; 33.7g protein; 5.3g fibre
tips you will need to buy a very small iceberg lettuce for this recipe. We used blue-eye fillets here, but you can substitute them with any firm white fish fillets you like.

Grilled prawns with tropical fruits

24 uncooked large king prawns (1.6kg)
¼ medium pineapple (300g), chopped coarsely
1 slightly firm large mango (600g), chopped coarsely
1 slightly firm large banana (230g), chopped coarsely
¼ cup loosely packed fresh mint leaves
2 tablespoons lime juice
herb sauce
½ cup loosely packed fresh mint leaves
½ cup loosely packed fresh flat-leaf parsley leaves
1 clove garlic, quartered
2 tablespoons lime juice
1 tablespoon olive oil

1 Cook prawns on heated oiled grill plate (or grill or barbecue) until changed in colour and cooked through.
2 Cook fruit on same grill plate until browned lightly.
3 Make herb sauce.
4 Combine prawns and fruit in large bowl with mint and juice. Divide prawn mixture among serving bowls; drizzle with sauce.
herb sauce blend or process ingredients until combined.

on the table in 30 minutes
serves 4 **per serving** 6.2g total fat (0.9g saturated fat); 1434kJ (343 cal); 25.0g carbohydrate; 43.8g protein; 4.5g fibre

Grilled scallops with papaya salsa

800g firm papaya, chopped coarsely
2 medium tomatoes (380g), seeded, chopped coarsely
1 medium red onion (170g), chopped coarsely
¼ cup (60ml) lime juice
1 fresh small red thai chilli, chopped finely
2 tablespoons coarsely chopped fresh coriander
1 tablespoon vegetable oil
36 scallops with roe

1 Combine papaya, tomato, onion, juice, chilli, coriander and oil in large bowl.
2 Cook scallops on heated oiled grill plate, in batches, until browned both sides.
3 Serve papaya salsa topped with scallops, accompanied by sweet chilli sauce, if desired.

on the table in 25 minutes
serves 4 **per serving** 6.4g total fat (1.0g saturated fat); 982kJ (235 cal); 14.1g carbohydrate; 27.8g protein; 4.2g fibre

Steamed asian bream

4 x 250g whole bream, cleaned
12cm piece fresh ginger (60g), cut into matchsticks
4 green onions, sliced thinly
4 small carrots (280g), cut into matchsticks
⅓ cup (80ml) tamari
1 tablespoon sesame oil

1 Preheat oven to 200°C/180°C fan-forced.
2 Fold 80cm-long piece of foil in half crossways; place fish onto foil, fill cavities with half of the combined ginger and vegetable mixture. Brush fish with combined tamari and oil; top with remaining ginger and vegetable mixture. Fold edges of foil to enclose fish.
3 Place fish parcel on oven tray; bake about 15 minutes or until fish is cooked as desired.
4 Serve fish sprinkled with fresh coriander leaves, if desired.

on the table in 30 minutes
serves 4 **per serving** 11.5g total fat (3.0g saturated fat); 999kJ (239 cal); 5.0g carbohydrate; 27.8g protein; 2.4g fibre
tips we used whole bream for this recipe, but any fairly small white-fleshed fish can be used. You need four 80cm-long sheets of foil to wrap the fish.

Stir-fried octopus with basil

1kg cleaned baby octopus
2 teaspoons peanut oil
2 teaspoons sesame oil
2 cloves garlic, crushed
2 fresh small red thai chillies, sliced thinly
2 large red capsicums (700g), sliced thinly
6 green onions, cut into 2cm lengths
¼ cup firmly packed fresh basil leaves
400g tat soi
2 tablespoons grated palm sugar
¼ cup (60ml) fish sauce
1 tablespoon kecap manis
¾ cup loosely packed fresh coriander leaves

1 Cut each octopus in half lengthways.
2 Heat peanut oil in wok; stir-fry octopus, in batches, until browned all over and tender. Cover to keep warm.
3 Heat sesame oil in wok; stir-fry garlic, chilli and capsicum until capsicum is just tender. Return octopus to wok with onion, basil, tat soi, sugar and sauces; stir-fry until tat soi just wilts. Remove from heat; stir in coriander.

on the table in 30 minutes
serves 4 **per serving** 10.2g total fat (1.7g saturated fat); 1919kJ (459 cal); 18.7g carbohydrate; 70.4g protein; 4.1g fibre

Oven-steamed ocean trout

4 x 240g ocean trout fillets
2 tablespoons lemon juice
1 tablespoon drained capers, chopped coarsely
2 teaspoons coarsely chopped fresh dill
1.2kg large new potatoes, sliced thickly

1 Preheat oven to 200°C/180°C fan-forced.
2 Place each fillet on a square piece of foil large enough to completely enclose fish; top each fillet with equal amounts of juice, capers and dill. Gather corners of foil squares together above fish, twist to enclose securely.
3 Place parcels on oven tray; cook about 15 minutes or until fish is cooked as desired.
4 Meanwhile, boil, steam or microwave potato until tender.
5 Just before serving, unwrap fish and remove from foil; serve with potatoes.

on the table in 25 minutes
serves 4 **per serving** 9.4g total fat (2.2g saturated fat); 1856kJ (444 cal); 31.0g carbohydrate; 52.8g protein; 4.1g fibre

Microwave prawn and pea risotto

600g cooked large prawns
20g butter
1 small leek (200g), sliced thinly
2 cloves garlic, crushed
8 saffron threads
2 cups (400g) arborio rice
2 cups (500ml) boiling water
1 cup (250ml) dry white wine
1½ cups (375ml) fish stock
1 cup (160g) frozen peas
2 tablespoons coarsely chopped fresh chives
¼ cup (60ml) lemon juice
30g butter, extra

1 Shell and devein prawns, leaving tails intact.
2 Place butter, leek, garlic and saffron in large microwave-safe bowl;
cook in microwave oven on high (100%), covered, about 2 minutes or
until leek softens. Stir in rice; cook on high (100%), covered, 1 minute.
Add the water, wine and stock; cook on high (100%), covered, 15 minutes,
pausing to stir three times during cooking.
3 Add peas and prawns (reserve a few for garnish, if desired); cook on
high (100%), covered, 3 minutes. Stir in chives, juice and extra butter.

on the table in 30 minutes
serves 4 **per serving** 11.7g total fat (7.0g saturated fat); 2512kJ
(601 cal); 84.0g carbohydrate; 26.4g protein; 4.3g fibre

Pepper-crusted swordfish with bean and potato salad

300g small red-skinned potatoes, halved
1 teaspoon ground white pepper
2 teaspoons cracked black pepper
½ cup (35g) stale breadcrumbs
4 x 200g swordfish fillets
200g green beans
200g yellow beans
¼ cup (60ml) lime juice
1 tablespoon olive oil
1 clove garlic, crushed

1 Boil, steam or microwave potato until just tender; drain. Cover to keep warm.
2 Combine peppers and breadcrumbs in small bowl; press mixture onto one side of each fillet. Cook fish, crumbed-side down, in heated oiled large frying pan, until browned lightly and crisp; turn, cook until browned lightly and cooked as desired.
3 Meanwhile, boil, steam or microwave beans until just tender; drain.
4 Place juice, oil and garlic in screw-top jar; shake well.
5 Place potato and beans in large bowl with dressing; toss gently to combine. Serve fish with salad.

on the table in 30 minutes
serves 4 **per serving** 9.6g total fat (2.1g saturated fat); 1450kJ (347 cal); 16.8g carbohydrate; 45.9g protein; 4.2g fibre

Sashimi stacks

½ lebanese cucumber (65g), seeded
½ medium avocado (125g)
400g piece sashimi salmon
1 teaspoon wasabi paste
4 green onions, quartered lengthways
½ sheet toasted seaweed (yaki-nori), cut into 1cm strips
2 teaspoons toasted sesame seeds
2 tablespoons japanese soy sauce

1 Cut cucumber and avocado into long thin strips.
2 Cut salmon into 32 thin slices.
3 Place 16 slices of the salmon on serving platter; spread each with
a little wasabi then divide cucumber, avocado and onion among slices.
Top each stack with one remaining salmon slice.
4 Wrap seaweed strip around each stack; sprinkle with sesame seeds.
Serve stacks with soy sauce.

on the table in 30 minutes
makes 16 **per stack** 3.2g total fat (0.7g saturated fat); 213kJ (51 cal);
0.3g carbohydrate; 5.3g protein; 0.3g fibre
tips use scissors to cut seaweed into strips. Use the freshest, sashimi-
quality fish you can find. Salmon sold as sashimi has to meet stringent
guidelines regarding its handling and treatment after leaving the water. We
suggest you seek local advice from authorities before eating raw seafood.

Seared tuna with chilled soba

200g dried soba noodles
¼ cup (60ml) mirin
2 tablespoons kecap manis
1 tablespoon cooking sake
2 teaspoons white sugar
5cm piece fresh ginger (25g), grated
1 clove garlic, crushed
4 x 200g tuna steaks
1 sheet toasted seaweed (yaki-nori), sliced thinly
2 green onions, chopped finely
1 teaspoon sesame oil
2 tablespoons pickled ginger, sliced thinly

1 Cook noodles in large saucepan of boiling water, uncovered, until just tender; drain. Rinse under cold water; drain. Place in medium bowl, cover; refrigerate until required.
2 Combine mirin, kecap manis, sake, sugar, fresh ginger and garlic in small jug.
3 Cook fish in heated oiled large frying pan, uncovered, until cooked as desired (tuna can become very dry if overcooked; we recommend you sear it over very high heat for about 30 seconds each side). Add mirin mixture to pan; coat fish both sides in mixture. Remove fish from pan; cover to keep warm.
4 Bring mixture in pan to a boil. Reduce heat, simmer, uncovered, 30 seconds. Strain sauce into small jug.
5 Place noodles in large bowl with seaweed, onion, oil and pickled ginger; toss gently to combine. Divide fish among plates, drizzle with sauce; top with noodles. Serve with wasabi, if desired.

on the table in 20 minutes
serves 4 **per serving** 13.2g total fat (4.9g saturated fat); 2182kJ (522 cal); 41.9g carbohydrate; 56.3g protein; 2.6g fibre

Prawn, scallop and asparagus salad with ginger dressing

400g uncooked medium king prawns
400g sea scallops
250g asparagus, trimmed, halved
⅓ cup coarsely chopped fresh chives
120g baby spinach leaves
1 large red capsicum (350g), chopped coarsely
ginger dressing
5cm piece fresh ginger (25g), grated
1 tablespoon olive oil
2 tablespoons lemon juice
1 teaspoon white sugar

1 Shell and devein prawns, leaving tails intact.
2 Cook prawns, scallops and asparagus, in batches, on heated oiled grill plate (or grill or barbecue) until cooked as desired.
3 Meanwhile, make ginger dressing.
4 Place prawns, scallops and asparagus in large bowl with chives, spinach, capsicum and dressing; toss gently to combine.
ginger dressing press ginger between two spoons over large bowl to extract juice; discard fibres. Whisk in oil, juice and sugar until combined.

on the table in 35 minutes
serves 4 **per serving** 5.9g total fat (0.9g saturated fat); 761kJ (182 cal); 5.9g carbohydrate; 24.9g protein; 2.5g fibre

Fish with thai-style dressing

100g snow pea sprouts, trimmed
1 cup loosely packed fresh mint leaves
½ cup loosely packed fresh coriander leaves
3 shallots (75g), sliced thinly
2 fresh long red chillies, sliced thinly
4 x 200g firm white fish fillets
thai-style dressing
⅓ cup (80ml) lime juice
2 tablespoons grated palm sugar
1 tablespoon fish sauce

1 Place sprouts, mint, coriander, shallots and chilli in medium bowl; toss gently to combine.
2 Cook fish on heated oiled grill plate (or grill or barbecue) until cooked as desired.
3 Meanwhile, make thai-style dressing.
4 Serve fish with salad, drizzled with dressing.
thai-style dressing place ingredients in screw-top jar; shake well.

on the table in 20 minutes
serves 4 **per serving** 1.6g total fat (0.3g saturated fat); 907kJ (217 cal); 13g carbohydrate; 36.8g protein; 2.6g fibre

Prawn, lime and rice noodle stir-fry

650g uncooked large prawns
375g thick dried rice stick noodles
1 tablespoon sesame oil
2 cloves garlic, crushed
2cm piece fresh ginger (10g), grated
2 fresh small red thai chillies, sliced thinly
250g broccolini, quartered
⅓ cup (80ml) lime juice
¼ cup (60ml) light soy sauce
2 teaspoons fish sauce
4 green onions, sliced thinly
2 tablespoons coarsely chopped fresh mint

1 Shell and devein prawns, leaving tails intact.
2 Place noodles in large heatproof bowl, cover with boiling water; stand until just tender, drain.
3 Heat oil in wok; stir-fry garlic, ginger and chilli until fragrant. Add broccolini; stir-fry until just tender. Add prawns; stir-fry until just changed in colour. Add noodles and remaining ingredients; stir-fry until hot.

on the table in 30 minutes
serves 4 **per serving** 6.4g total fat (0.7g saturated fat); 1597kJ (382 cal); 52.2g carbohydrate; 25.8g protein; 4.5g fibre

Squid stuffed with smoked trout and basil

1 small red onion (100g)
300g hot-smoked ocean trout fillets, flaked coarsely
1 cup coarsely chopped fresh basil
8 baby squid hoods (500g), cleaned
100g baby rocket leaves
½ cup loosely packed fresh flat-leaf parsley leaves
1 cup coarsely chopped fresh mint
¼ cup (60ml) white wine vinegar
1 tablespoon olive oil
2 limes, cut into 8 wedges

1 Slice half of the onion thinly; chop remaining half finely.
2 Combine chopped onion, fish and half of the basil in small bowl;
fill hoods with fish mixture up to about 2cm from opening, secure
with toothpicks.
3 Cook squid in heated lightly oiled large frying pan, uncovered, until
browned lightly all over and tender.
4 Place rocket, parsley, mint, sliced onion and remaining basil in large
bowl with combined vinegar and oil; toss gently to combine.
5 Cut squid in half on the diagonal; divide pieces among plates with
salad and lime wedges.

on the table in 30 minutes
serves 4 **per serving** 10.3g total fat (2.1g saturated fat); 1158kJ
(277 cal); 2.6g carbohydrate; 41.7g protein; 3g fibre

Crisp-skinned snapper with stir-fried vegetables and black beans

½ teaspoon sea salt
1 teaspoon coarsely ground black pepper
4 x 200g snapper fillets
1 teaspoon sesame oil
1 large brown onion (200g), cut into thin wedges
1 clove garlic, crushed
1cm piece fresh ginger (5g), grated
1 tablespoon salted black beans, rinsed, drained
1 medium green capsicum (200g), chopped coarsely
1 medium red capsicum (200g), chopped coarsely
6 green onions, sliced thickly
100g snow peas
100g broccolini, chopped coarsely
½ cup (125ml) water
¼ cup (60ml) oyster sauce
2 tablespoons lemon juice
500g baby buk choy, chopped coarsely
1 cup (80g) bean sprouts

1 Combine salt and pepper in small bowl; rub into skin side of each fillet. Cook fish, skin-side down, on heated lightly oiled grill plate (or grill or barbecue) until browned and crisp; turn, cook until browned and cooked as desired. Cover to keep warm.
2 Meanwhile, heat oil in wok; stir-fry brown onion, garlic and ginger until onion softens. Add beans; stir-fry 1 minute. Add capsicums, green onion, snow peas and broccolini; stir-fry until vegetables are just tender.
3 Stir in the water, sauce and juice; cook, stirring, until mixture thickens slightly. Add buk choy and bean sprouts; stir-fry until heated through. Serve fish on vegetables.

on the table in 25 minutes
serves 4 **per serving** 5.2g total fat (1.4g saturated fat); 1279kJ (306 cal); 13.7g carbohydrate; 47.6g protein; 6.0g fibre

Barbecued chilli prawns with fresh mango salad

1kg uncooked large king prawns
½ teaspoon ground turmeric
1 teaspoon chilli powder
2 teaspoons sweet paprika
2 cloves garlic, crushed
mango salad
2 large mangoes (1.2kg), chopped coarsely
1 small red onion (100g), sliced thinly
1 fresh long red chilli, sliced thinly
1½ cups (120g) bean sprouts
½ cup coarsely chopped fresh coriander
2 teaspoons fish sauce
2 teaspoons grated palm sugar
2 tablespoons lime juice
1 tablespoon peanut oil

1 Shell and devein prawns, leaving tails intact. Combine prawns with turmeric, chilli, paprika and garlic in large bowl.
2 Cook prawn mixture, in batches, on heated oiled grill plate (or grill or barbecue) until browned lightly.
3 Make mango salad; serve with prawns.
mango salad place ingredients in medium bowl; toss gently to combine.

on the table in 35 minutes
serves 4 **per serving** 5.9g total fat (1g saturated fat); 1229kJ (294 cal); 30.3g carbohydrate; 29.5g protein; 5.1g fibre

Asian-flavoured trout with shiitake mushrooms

1 tablespoon salted black beans, rinsed, drained
1 clove garlic, crushed
3cm piece fresh ginger (15g), grated
1 teaspoon dried chilli flakes
⅓ cup (80ml) soy sauce
6 green onions, sliced thinly
4 x 500g whole rainbow trout
400g fresh shiitake mushrooms
2 tablespoons lemon juice

1 Crush beans in small bowl. Add garlic, ginger, chilli, half of the soy sauce and half of the onion; stir to combine.
2 Place each fish on oiled piece of foil large enough to completely enclose it; place a quarter of the bean mixture inside each fish, wrap tightly in foil. Cook fish on heated oiled grill plate, uncovered, about 10 minutes or until cooked as desired.
3 Meanwhile, cook mushrooms on heated oiled flat plate, uncovered, until tender; drizzle with remaining soy sauce.
4 Serve mushrooms with fish, drizzled with juice and sprinkled with remaining onion.

on the table in 25 minutes
serves 4 **per serving** 7.6g total fat (1.7g saturated fat); 1074kJ (257 cal); 2.7g carbohydrate; 42.2g protein; 3.3g fibre

Grilled blue-eye with gai lan

4 x 200g blue-eye fillets
800g gai lan, chopped coarsely
ginger and garlic dressing
8cm piece fresh ginger (40g), grated
2 cloves garlic, crushed
⅓ cup (80ml) water
⅓ cup (80ml) tamari

1 Cook fish in heated lightly oiled large frying pan, uncovered, until cooked through.
2 Meanwhile, boil, steam or microwave gai lan until tender; drain.
3 Make ginger and garlic dressing.
4 Serve fish with gai lan; drizzle with dressing.
ginger and garlic dressing place ingredients in screw-top jar; shake well.

on the table in 25 minutes
serves 4 **per serving** 1.7g total fat (0.2g saturated fat); 828kJ (198 cal); 3.5g carbohydrate; 41.2g protein; 8.2g fibre
tip we used blue-eye for this recipe, but you can use any firm white-fleshed fish fillets.

Char-grilled tuna salad

600g tuna steak
2 medium red capsicums (400g), sliced thinly
200g mesclun
dressing
¼ cup (60ml) mirin
1 tablespoon light soy sauce
1 clove garlic, crushed
1 fresh small red thai chilli, chopped finely
1 green onion, chopped finely

1 Cook tuna on heated oiled grill plate (or grill or barbecue) until browned both sides and cooked as desired. Cover, rest 2 minutes; cut into thick slices.
2 Meanwhile, make dressing.
3 Place tuna in large bowl with capsicum, mesclun and dressing; toss gently to combine.
dressing place ingredients in screw-top jar; shake well.

on the table in 15 minutes
serves 4 **per serving** 8.9g total fat (3.5g saturated fat); 1141kJ (273 cal); 4.6g carbohydrate; 40.1g protein; 2.2g fibre

Scallops with sugar snap pea salad

250g sugar snap peas, trimmed
20 scallops on the half shell (800g), roe removed
100g cherry tomatoes, halved
1 medium lebanese cucumber (130g), seeded, sliced thinly
½ cup loosely packed fresh mint leaves

balsamic dressing
1 teaspoon finely grated lemon rind
2 tablespoons lemon juice
1 clove garlic, crushed
1 tablespoon olive oil
2 teaspoons balsamic vinegar

lemon dressing
1 tablespoon finely grated lemon rind
¼ cup (60ml) lemon juice
1 clove garlic, crushed
1 tablespoon olive oil

1 Boil, steam or microwave peas until just tender; drain.
2 Remove scallops from shell; reserve shells. Place scallops, in single layer, in large steamer fitted over large saucepan of boiling water; steam scallops, covered, about 4 minutes or until cooked as desired.
3 Rinse and dry scallop shells.
4 Meanwhile, make balsamic dressing. Make lemon dressing.
5 Place peas in medium bowl with tomato, cucumber, mint and balsamic dressing; toss gently to combine.
6 Return scallops to shells; drizzle with lemon dressing. Serve scallops with salad.
balsamic dressing place ingredients in screw-top jar; shake well.
lemon dressing place ingredients in screw-top jar; shake well.

on the table in 25 minutes
serves 4 **per serving** 10.3g total fat (1.6g saturated fat); 786kJ (188 cal); 5.6g carbohydrate; 16.9g protein; 2.8g fibre

Seared ocean trout with buk choy

1 litre (4 cups) water
¼ cup (60ml) soy sauce
1 star anise
1 teaspoon sambal oelek
1 tablespoon honey
800g baby buk choy, halved lengthways
1 tablespoon sesame oil
4 x 240g ocean trout fillets

1 Combine the water, sauce, star anise, sambal and honey in medium saucepan; bring to a boil. Cook buk choy in boiling stock until just wilted. Remove buk choy; cover to keep warm. Strain stock into medium bowl; discard solids. Return stock to heat; boil, uncovered, while cooking fish.
2 Heat oil in large frying pan; sear fish over high heat until cooked as desired. Serve fish on buk choy; drizzle with stock.

on the table in 25 minutes
serves 4 **per serving** 14.2g total fat (2.8g saturated fat); 1534kJ (367 cal); 8.5g carbohydrate; 49.6g protein; 2.7g fibre

Balmain bugs and citrus salad

2kg uncooked balmain bugs
1 tablespoon olive oil
2 tablespoons orange juice
2 teaspoons finely grated orange rind
1 tablespoon wholegrain mustard
citrus salad
1 medium grapefruit (425g)
1 large orange (300g)
1 lemon (140g)
150g curly endive, chopped coarsely
1 large fennel bulb (550g), trimmed, sliced thinly
1 tablespoon wholegrain mustard
1 tablespoon olive oil

1 Place balmain bugs upside down on chopping board; cut tail from body, discard body. Halve tail lengthways; discard back vein. Cook bugs on heated oiled grill plate (or grill or barbecue), uncovered, until cooked through.
2 Meanwhile, make citrus salad.
3 Place bugs in large bowl with combined oil, juice, rind and mustard; toss bugs to coat in mixture. Serve with citrus salad.
citrus salad cut unpeeled grapefruit, orange and lemon into equal size wedges; cook on heated oiled grill plate, uncovered, until browned. Place fruit in large bowl with endive, fennel and combined mustard and oil; toss gently to combine.

on the table in 35 minutes
serves 4 **per serving** 11.1g total fat (1.6g saturated fat); 1300kJ (311 cal); 13.7g carbohydrate; 36.2g protein; 5.4g fibre
tip large king prawns or scampi are good substitutes for the bugs in this recipe.

Fish with herb and tomato dressing

12 baby new potatoes (480g), halved
4 medium zucchini (480g), quartered
2 tablespoons olive oil
4 white fish fillets (800g)
2 medium egg tomatoes (150g), chopped finely
2 tablespoons lemon juice
1 tablespoon finely chopped fresh dill
2 tablespoons finely chopped fresh basil

1 Boil, steam or microwave potato and zucchini, separately, until tender; drain.
2 Meanwhile, heat half of the oil in large frying pan; cook fish until cooked as desired. Remove from pan; cover to keep warm.
3 Heat remaining oil in same cleaned pan; cook tomato and juice, stirring, 2 minutes. Remove from heat; stir in herbs.
4 Divide fish and vegetables among plates; drizzle with tomato mixture.

on the table in 30 minutes
serves 4 **per serving** 10.8g total fat (1.5g saturated fat); 1371kJ (328 cal); 18.5g carbohydrate; 38.1g protein; 4.6g fibre
tip we used blue-eye in this recipe, but you can use any firm white fish, such as perch or ling.

Prawn tamarind stir-fry with buk choy

1kg uncooked medium king prawns
2 tablespoons peanut oil
4 green onions, sliced thinly lengthways
4 cloves garlic, sliced thinly
1 teaspoon cornflour
½ cup (125ml) vegetable stock
2 tablespoons oyster sauce
1 tablespoon tamarind puree
1 teaspoon sambal oelek
2 teaspoons sesame oil
1 tablespoon lime juice
1 tablespoon brown sugar
350g yellow patty-pan squash, sliced thickly
300g sugar snap peas, trimmed
800g baby buk choy, chopped coarsely

1 Shell and devein prawns, leaving tails intact.
2 Heat half of the peanut oil in wok; stir-fry onion and garlic, separately, until browned lightly. Drain on absorbent paper.
3 Blend cornflour and stock in small jug; stir in sauce, tamarind, sambal, sesame oil, juice and sugar.
4 Heat remaining peanut oil in wok; stir-fry prawns, in batches, until changed in colour and almost cooked through.
5 Stir-fry squash in wok until just tender. Add cornflour mixture; stir-fry until sauce boils and thickens slightly.
6 Return prawns to wok with peas and buk choy; stir-fry until buk choy just wilts and prawns are cooked through.
7 Serve stir-fry with steamed jasmine rice, if desired, and topped with reserved onion and garlic.

on the table in 35 minutes
serves 4 **per serving** 13.3g total fat (2.2g saturated fat); 1375kJ (329 cal); 15.6g carbohydrate; 33.2g protein; 7.0g fibre

279

Sumac, salt and pepper fish with mediterranean salad

1 cup (200g) couscous
1 cup (250ml) boiling water
1 tablespoon olive oil
4 x 200g blue-eye fillets
2 tablespoons sumac
1 teaspoon salt
1 teaspoon cracked black pepper
1 lemon, quartered
mediterranean salad
2 medium tomatoes (300g), seeded, chopped coarsely
2 medium red capsicums (400g), chopped coarsely
2 tablespoons seeded kalamata olives, chopped coarsely
2 tablespoons drained baby capers, rinsed
1 cup coarsely chopped fresh flat-leaf parsley

1 Combine couscous with the water in large heatproof bowl. Cover; stand about 5 minutes or until water is absorbed, fluffing with fork occasionally. Stir in oil.
2 Meanwhile, combine fish with sumac, salt and pepper in large bowl. Cook fish, in batches, in heated lightly oiled large frying pan until cooked as desired.
3 Make mediterranean salad.
4 Divide couscous among plates, top with salad and fish; serve with lemon.
mediterranean salad place ingredients in medium bowl; toss gently to combine.

on the table in 30 minutes
serves 4 **per serving** 9.7g total fat (2.1g saturated fat); 1990kJ (476 cal); 45.7g carbohydrate; 49.9g protein; 3.9g fibre
tip we used blue-eye for this recipe, but you can use any firm white-fleshed fish fillets.

chicken

Kebabs with papaya salsa

12 chicken tenderloins (900g)
1 small papaya (650g), peeled, seeded
4 green onions, sliced thinly
1 lebanese cucumber (130g), seeded, chopped coarsely
½ cup firmly packed, coarsely chopped fresh mint
2cm piece fresh ginger (10g), grated
1 tablespoon sweet chilli sauce
2 tablespoons lime juice

1 Thread chicken onto skewers. Cook skewers, in batches, on heated oiled grill plate (or grill or barbecue) about 15 minutes or until chicken is browned all over and cooked through.
2 Meanwhile, chop papaya finely. Place in small bowl with onion, cucumber, mint, ginger, sauce and juice; toss gently to combine.
3 Serve kebabs topped with salsa.

on the table in 25 minutes
serves 4 **per serving** 5.6g total fat (1.4g saturated fat); 1292kJ (309 cal); 10.2g carbohydrate; 51.9g protein; 3.8g fibre
tips soak 12 bamboo skewers in water before use to avoid them scorching and splintering. You can substitute mango for the papaya, if you like.

Thai chicken and rice

2 cups (300g) long-grain white rice
1 cup firmly packed fresh mint leaves
⅓ cup (80ml) sweet chilli sauce
1 tablespoon fish sauce
1 tablespoon soy sauce
½ cup (125ml) lime juice
2cm piece fresh ginger (10g), grated
2 x 10cm sticks (40g) finely chopped fresh lemon grass
4 x 170g chicken breast fillets
1 small red capsicum (150g), chopped finely

1 Cook rice in large saucepan of boiling water, uncovered, until just tender; drain.
2 Meanwhile, reserve 2 tablespoons of the mint; blend or process remaining mint with sauces, juice, ginger and lemon grass until smooth.
3 Cook chicken, in batches, on heated oiled grill plate (or grill or barbecue) until browned both sides and cooked through.
4 Toss capsicum through cooked rice. Divide among serving plates; top with chicken. Drizzle with sauce; sprinkle with reserved coarsely chopped mint.

on the table in 20 minutes
serves 4 **per serving** 5.1g total fat (1.2g saturated fat); 2103kJ (503 cal); 65.9g carbohydrate; 45.4g protein; 3.0g fibre

Chicken, vegetable and rice noodle stir-fry

500g fresh wide rice noodles
1 tablespoon sesame oil
500g chicken breast fillets, sliced thinly
250g oyster mushrooms, sliced thinly
¼ cup (60ml) oyster sauce
1 tablespoon fish sauce
1 tablespoon white sugar
2 teaspoons sambal oelek
250g baby spinach leaves
¼ cup coarsely chopped fresh coriander

1 Rinse noodles in strainer under hot water. Separate noodles with fork; drain.
2 Heat oil in wok; stir-fry chicken, in batches, until browned all over and cooked through.
3 Place mushrooms in wok; stir-fry until just tender. Return chicken to wok with noodles, sauces, sugar and sambal; stir-fry until heated through.
4 Remove wok from heat. Add baby spinach and coriander; toss gently to combine.

on the table in 20 minutes
serves 4 **per serving** 8.6g total fat (1.4g saturated fat); 1572kJ (376 cal); 36.4g carbohydrate; 35.2g protein; 5.3g fibre

Shredded chicken salad

500g chicken breast fillets
125g rice vermicelli noodles
1 large carrot (180g), cut into matchsticks
1 medium red capsicum (200g), sliced thinly
1 medium green capsicum (200g), sliced thinly
1 lebanese cucumber (130g), seeded, sliced thinly
1 fresh long red chilli, sliced thinly
1 cup coarsely shredded fresh mint
¼ cup (35g) toasted unsalted peanuts, chopped coarsely
lime and palm sugar dressing
¼ cup (60ml) lime juice
¼ cup (65g) grated palm sugar
¼ cup (60ml) fish sauce

1 Make lime and palm sugar dressing.
2 Place chicken and half of the dressing in medium saucepan with barely enough boiling water to cover chicken; bring to a boil. Reduce heat; simmer, uncovered, about 10 minutes or until chicken is cooked through. Cool chicken in poaching liquid 10 minutes; discard liquid (or reserve for another use). Using two forks, shred chicken finely.
3 Meanwhile, place vermicelli in large healproof bowl; cover with boiling water. Stand until just tender; drain. Rinse under cold water; drain.
4 Place chicken and vermicelli in large bowl with carrot, capsicums, cucumber, chilli, mint and remaining dressing; toss gently to combine. Divide salad among plates; top with nuts.
lime and palm sugar dressing place ingredients in screw-top jar; shake well.

on the table in 35 minutes
serves 4 **per serving** 7.8g total fat (1.3g saturated fat); 1613kJ (386 cal); 43.1g carbohydrate; 35.6g protein; 4.6g fibre

Glazed-chicken tortilla with sprout and herb salad

¼ cup (80g) cranberry sauce
1 tablespoon wholegrain mustard
1 tablespoon lemon juice
5cm piece fresh ginger (25g), grated
1 clove garlic, crushed
500g chicken breast fillets
1 small red onion (100g), sliced thinly
60g snow pea sprouts
¼ cup thinly sliced fresh coriander
¼ cup thinly sliced fresh mint
1 tablespoon white wine vinegar
4 large flour tortillas

1 Heat combined sauce, mustard, juice, ginger and garlic in small saucepan, stirring, until glaze comes to a boil.
2 Cook chicken, in batches, in heated lightly oiled large frying pan, brushing frequently with glaze, until cooked through. Cover chicken; stand 5 minutes before slicing thickly.
3 Meanwhile, place onion, sprouts, herbs and vinegar in medium bowl; toss gently to combine.
4 Heat tortillas according to manufacturer's instructions.
5 Divide chicken and salad among centres of tortillas; roll tortillas around filling to form cone shapes.

on the table in 35 minutes
serves 4 **per serving** 5.6g total fat (1.2g saturated fat); 1296kJ (310 cal); 31g carbohydrate; 33.4g protein; 2.9g fibre

Chicken tenderloins in green peppercorn and tarragon dressing

4 medium potatoes (800g)
8 chicken tenderloins (600g)
1 tablespoon cracked black pepper
4 large tomatoes (1kg), sliced thinly
1 medium red onion (170g), sliced thinly
green peppercorn and tarragon dressing
2 tablespoons water
2 teaspoons drained green peppercorns, crushed
2 teaspoons wholegrain mustard
2 green onions, sliced thinly
1 tablespoon coarsely chopped fresh tarragon
1 tablespoon olive oil
1 tablespoon white sugar
⅓ cup (80ml) white wine vinegar

1 Boil, steam or microwave potatoes until just tender; drain.
2 Meanwhile, combine chicken and pepper in large bowl. Cook chicken, in batches, on heated oiled grill plate (or grill or barbecue) until browned both sides and cooked through. Stand 5 minutes; slice thickly.
3 When potatoes are cool enough to handle, slice thickly. Cook potato, in batches, on same heated oiled grill plate until browned both sides.
4 Make green peppercorn and tarragon dressing.
5 Arrange chicken, potato, tomato and onion slices on serving plates; drizzle with dressing.
green peppercorn and tarragon dressing combine the water, peppercorn, mustard, green onion, tarragon, oil, sugar and vinegar in small bowl. Whisk to combine.

on the table in 25 minutes
serves 4 **per serving** 8.5g total fat (1.5g saturated fat); 1668kJ (399 cal); 35.2g carbohydrate; 41.5g protein; 6.6g fibre

Chicken and mixed pea stir-fry

1½ cups (300g) jasmine rice
1 tablespoon peanut oil
700g chicken breast fillets, sliced thinly
1 medium brown onion (150g), sliced thinly
1 fresh long red chilli, sliced thinly
1 clove garlic, crushed
150g sugar snap peas, trimmed
150g snow peas, trimmed
125g fresh baby corn, halved
2 tablespoons kecap manis
2 tablespoons char siu sauce
½ cup (125ml) chicken stock
1 tablespoon cornflour
2 tablespoons lime juice

1 Cook rice in large saucepan of boiling water, uncovered, until just tender; drain. Cover to keep warm.
2 Meanwhile, heat half of the oil in wok; stir-fry chicken, in batches, until browned and almost cooked through.
3 Heat remaining oil in wok; stir-fry onion, chilli and garlic until onion softens. Add peas and corn; stir-fry until vegetables are just tender. Return chicken to wok with sauces and stock; stir-fry about 2 minutes or until chicken is cooked through. Stir in blended cornflour and juice; stir-fry until sauce boils and thickens. Divide rice among serving plates; top with stir-fry.

on the table in 35 minutes
serves 4 **per serving** 10.3g total fat (2.1g saturated fat); 2562kJ (613 cal); 76.6g carbohydrate; 49.6g protein; 5.3g fibre

Chilli-chicken stir-fry with asian greens

2½ cups (500g) jasmine rice
1 tablespoon sesame oil
4 chicken breast fillets (800g), sliced thinly
2 cloves garlic, crushed
1 large red capsicum (350g), sliced thinly
⅓ cup (100g) thai chilli jam
2 tablespoons sweet chilli sauce
¼ cup (60ml) chicken stock
500g baby buk choy, halved lengthways
225g can water chestnuts, drained, halved
4 green onions, sliced thinly
1 tablespoon sesame seeds, toasted

1 Cook rice in large saucepan of boiling water, uncovered, until just tender; drain. Cover to keep warm.
2 Meanwhile, heat half of the oil in wok; stir-fry chicken, in batches, until cooked through. Return chicken to wok with garlic, capsicum, jam, sauce and stock; stir-fry about 2 minutes or until sauce thickens slightly. Remove from wok.
3 Heat remaining oil in same cleaned wok; stir-fry buk choy, chestnuts and onion until buk choy just wilts. Divide buk choy mixture among serving plates; top with chilli chicken, sprinkle with sesame seeds. Serve with rice.

on the table in 25 minutes
serves 4 **per serving** 13.7g total fat (2.7g saturated fat); 3490kJ (835 cal); 115.9g carbohydrate; 57.6g protein; 5.4g fibre

Harissa chicken with couscous salad

800g chicken breast fillets, sliced thickly
2 tablespoons harissa
2 teaspoons finely grated lemon rind
couscous salad
1 ½ cups (375ml) chicken stock
2 teaspoons ground coriander
1 ½ cups (300g) couscous
1 medium red capsicum (200g), chopped finely
1 medium brown onion (150g), chopped finely
3 green onions, sliced thinly
½ cup firmly packed fresh coriander leaves
⅓ cup (80ml) lemon juice
1 tablespoon olive oil

1 Combine chicken with harissa and rind in medium bowl.
2 Cook chicken on heated oiled grill plate (or grill or barbecue), uncovered, until cooked through. Cover chicken; stand 5 minutes, slice thickly.
3 Meanwhile, make couscous salad. Serve chicken on salad.
couscous salad bring stock and ground coriander to a boil in medium saucepan. Remove from heat; stir in couscous. Cover; stand 5 minutes or until liquid is absorbed, fluffing occasionally with fork. Add remaining ingredients; toss gently to combine.

on the table in 30 minutes
serves 4 **per serving** 10.4g total fat (2.2g saturated fat); 2475kJ (592 cal); 64.7g carbohydrate; 57.4g protein; 2.3g fibre
tip harissa, a North African paste made from dried red chillies, garlic, olive oil and caraway seeds, can be used as a rub for meat, an ingredient in sauces and dressings, or eaten on its own, as a condiment. It is available ready-made from Middle-Eastern food shops and some supermarkets.

Lemon grass and asparagus chicken

500g chicken breast fillets, sliced thickly
3 cloves garlic, crushed
2 x 10cm sticks (40g) finely chopped fresh lemon grass
1 teaspoon white sugar
1cm piece fresh ginger (5g), grated
1 tablespoon peanut oil
400g asparagus, trimmed
1 large brown onion (200g), sliced thickly
2 medium tomatoes (380g), seeded, chopped coarsely
2 teaspoons finely chopped fresh coriander
2 tablespoons roasted sesame seeds

1 Combine chicken with garlic, lemon grass, sugar, ginger and half of the oil in medium bowl.
2 Cut asparagus spears into thirds; boil, steam or microwave until just tender. Rinse immediately under cold water; drain.
3 Heat remaining oil in wok; stir-fry onion until just soft, remove from wok.
4 Stir-fry chicken mixture, in batches, until chicken is browned and cooked through.
5 Return chicken mixture and onion to wok with asparagus and tomato; stir-fry until heated through. Serve sprinkled with coriander and seeds.

on the table in 30 minutes
serves 4 **per serving** 7.6g total fat (1.6g saturated fat); 928kJ (222 cal); 5.7g carbohydrate; 31.2g protein; 2.5g fibre

Chicken, lemon and artichoke skewers

3 medium lemons (420g)
3 small red onions (300g)
500g chicken breast fillets, cut into 3cm pieces
400g can marinated quartered artichoke hearts, drained
300g button mushrooms
100g baby rocket leaves
2 tablespoons drained baby capers, rinsed, drained
lemon dressing
1 tablespoon lemon juice
2 cloves garlic, crushed
½ teaspoon mild english mustard
1 tablespoon white wine vinegar
1 tablespoon olive oil

1 Cut each lemon into eight wedges; cut two of the onions into six wedges. Thread lemon and onion wedges, chicken, artichokes and mushrooms, alternately, onto skewers.
2 Make lemon dressing.
3 Place skewers in shallow dish; brush with half of the dressing. Cook skewers on heated lightly oiled grill plate (or grill or barbecue) until cooked through.
4 Meanwhile, slice remaining onion thinly, place in large bowl with rocket, capers and remaining dressing; toss gently to combine. Divide salad among serving plates; top each with three skewers.
lemon dressing place ingredients in screw-top jar; shake well.

on the table in 35 minutes
serves 4 **per serving** 8.3g total fat (1.4g saturated fat); 1078kJ (258 cal); 7.6g carbohydrate; 34.5g protein; 7.0g fibre
tip soak 12 bamboo skewers in water before use to avoid them scorching and splintering.

Chicken and tamarind stir-fry

2 cups (400g) jasmine rice
700g chicken breast fillets, sliced thinly
1 tablespoon tamarind concentrate
3 cloves garlic, crushed
2 fresh small red thai chillies, sliced thinly
2 teaspoons white sugar
1 tablespoon lime juice
1 tablespoon peanut oil
1 large brown onion (200g), sliced thickly
½ cup loosely packed fresh coriander leaves

1 Cook rice in large saucepan of boiling water, uncovered, until just tender; drain.
2 Meanwhile, combine chicken, tamarind, garlic, chilli, sugar and juice in medium bowl.
3 Heat half of the oil in wok; stir-fry chicken mixture, in batches, until browned all over and cooked through.
4 Heat remaining oil in wok; stir-fry onion until just softened. Return chicken to wok; toss gently to combine. Serve with rice; sprinkle with coriander.

on the table in 25 minutes
serves 4 **per serving** 9.2g total fat (2.0g saturated fat); 2579kJ (617 cal); 84.1g carbohydrate; 47.0g protein; 1.9g fibre

Char-grilled chicken with warm tomato salad

4 x 170g chicken breast fillets
2 tablespoons lime juice
¼ cup (60ml) sweet chilli sauce
2 cloves garlic, crushed
4 fresh kaffir lime leaves, shredded
20g butter
2 medium brown onions (300g), sliced thickly
2 tablespoons red wine vinegar
¼ cup (55g) white sugar
2 tablespoons sweet chilli sauce, extra
¼ cup (60ml) water
¼ cup (60ml) orange juice
6 medium egg tomatoes (450g), cut into wedges
1 tablespoon bottled jalapeño chillies, chopped coarsely
3 green onions, sliced thickly

1 Combine chicken with juice, sauce, garlic and leaves in large bowl.
2 Heat butter in large saucepan; cook brown onion, stirring, until just softened. Add vinegar and sugar; cook, stirring, 2 minutes. Stir in extra sauce, the water and juice; add tomato and chilli, stir until heated through.
3 Cook drained chicken, in batches, on heated oiled grill plate (or grill or barbecue) until browned both sides and cooked through. Cover to keep warm.
4 Serve chicken on warm tomato salad; top with green onion.

on the table in 30 minutes
serves 4 **per serving** 9.0g total fat (3.9g saturated fat); 1517kJ (363 cal); 26.7g carbohydrate; 41.2g protein; 3.9g fibre

Chicken with buk choy and flat mushrooms

2 tablespoons honey
⅓ cup (80ml) soy sauce
2 tablespoons dry sherry
1 teaspoon five-spice powder
4cm piece fresh ginger (20g), grated
1 tablespoon peanut oil
4 x 170g single chicken breast fillets
4 flat mushrooms (360g)
500g baby buk choy, quartered lengthways
1 cup (250ml) chicken stock
2 teaspoons cornflour
2 tablespoons water

1 Combine honey, sauce, sherry, five-spice, ginger and oil in small jug. Combine chicken with half of the honey mixture in medium bowl. Cover; refrigerate 10 minutes.
2 Meanwhile, cook mushrooms and buk choy, in batches, on heated lightly oiled grill plate (or grill or barbecue) until just tender; cover to keep warm.
3 Cook drained chicken on same lightly oiled grill plate (or grill or barbecue) until browned both sides and cooked through. Cover; stand 5 minutes then slice thickly.
4 Combine remaining honey mixture in small saucepan with stock; bring to a boil. Stir in blended cornflour and water; cook, stirring, until sauce boils and thickens slightly.
5 Divide mushrooms and buk choy among serving plates; top with chicken, drizzle with sauce.

on the table in 25 minutes
serves 4 **per serving** 9.3g total fat (2.0g saturated fat); 1442kJ (345 cal); 15.7g carbohydrate; 44.9g protein; 4.0g fibre

Chicken with cucumber and tomato salsa

4 x 170g chicken breast fillets
2 small tomatoes (260g), seeded, sliced thinly
1 lebanese cucumber (130g), seeded, sliced thinly
1 small red onion (100g), halved, sliced thinly
2 tablespoons sweet chilli sauce
3 teaspoons lime juice
1 tablespoon coarsely chopped fresh coriander

1 Cook chicken, in batches, on heated oiled grill plate (or grill or barbecue) until browned both sides and cooked through.
2 Combine remaining ingredients in small bowl; toss gently to combine.
3 Serve chicken topped with salsa.

on the table in 25 minutes
serves 4 **per serving** 4.3g total fat (1.1g saturated fat); 907kJ (217 cal); 4.3g carbohydrate; 39.3g protein; 1.4g fibre

Chicken skewers with chilli and lime sauce

⅓ cup (80ml) sweet chilli sauce
2 tablespoons fish sauce
2 tablespoons lime juice
6 chicken thigh fillets (660g), halved lengthways
1 green onion, sliced thinly

1 Combine sauces and juice in small bowl; reserve half of the sauce in small serving bowl.
2 Thread chicken onto skewers lengthways; brush chicken with remaining sauce. Cook skewers on heated oiled grill plate (or grill or barbecue) until cooked through.
3 Add onion to reserved sauce; serve with skewers.

on the table in 25 minutes
serves 4 **per serving** 12.1g total fat (3.6g saturated fat); 1108kJ (265 cal); 7.3g carbohydrate; 31.6g protein; 0.2g fibre
tip soak 12 bamboo skewers in water before use to avoid them scorching and splintering.

meat

Chilli rice noodles with buk choy

400g fresh thin rice noodles
1 tablespoon peanut oil
500g lamb mince
3 cloves garlic, crushed
2 fresh small red thai chillies, chopped finely
400g buk choy, sliced thinly
2 tablespoons tamari
1 tablespoon fish sauce
2 tablespoons kecap manis
4 green onions, sliced thinly
1 cup firmly packed fresh thai basil leaves
3 cups (240g) bean sprouts

1 Place noodles in medium heatproof bowl; cover with boiling water, separate with fork, drain.
2 Heat oil in wok; stir-fry lamb until browned. Add garlic and chilli; stir-fry until fragrant. Add noodles, buk choy, tamari, sauce and kecap manis; stir-fry until buk choy just wilts.
3 Remove from heat; stir in onion, basil and sprouts.

on the table in 35 minutes
serves 4 **per serving** 14.4g total fat (4.7g saturated fat); 1877kJ (449 cal); 44.5g carbohydrate; 34.3g protein; 5.3g fibre

Mulled-wine pork and stone fruits

2 cups (500ml) water
1 cup (250ml) dry white wine
½ cup (110g) white sugar
2 cinnamon sticks
5 cloves
¼ cup (60ml) brandy
2 medium peaches (300g), stoned, quartered
4 medium plums (450g), stoned, quartered
2 medium nectarines (340g), stoned, quartered
4 medium apricots (200g), stoned, quartered
800g pork fillets, trimmed
1 fresh long red chilli, sliced thinly
1 long green chilli, sliced thinly

1 Combine the water, wine and sugar in heated large frying pan, stirring constantly, without boiling, until sugar dissolves; bring to a boil. Add cinnamon, cloves, brandy and fruit, reduce heat; simmer, uncovered, about 5 minutes or until fruit is just tender. Using slotted spoon, transfer fruit to large bowl; cover to keep warm.
2 Return poaching liquid to a boil; add pork. Reduce heat, simmer, covered, about 10 minutes or until pork is just cooked through. Cool pork in liquid 10 minutes then slice thickly. Discard poaching liquid.
3 Combine chillies with fruit; divide fruit and any fruit juices among serving bowls, top with pork.

on the table in 30 minutes
serves 4 **per serving** 4.9g total fat (1.6g saturated fat); 2094kJ (501 cal); 46.5g carbohydrate; 46.2g protein; 5.5g fibre
tip "mulled" wine has been heated and spiced, and is a favourite winter drink in cold climates. Here, we've used the best of the summer's stone-fruit crop to prove that mulled wine can be consumed any time of year!

Moroccan beef salad

1 cup (250ml) vegetable stock
1½ cups (300g) couscous
½ cup (75g) thinly sliced dried apricots
½ cup (80g) sultanas
1 medium red onion (170g), chopped finely
¼ cup finely chopped fresh mint
2 tablespoons coarsely chopped fresh dill
600g beef rump steak
1 tablespoon toasted pine nuts
2 teaspoons cumin seeds
¾ cup (180ml) oil-free french dressing

1 Bring stock to a boil in medium saucepan; remove from heat. Add couscous to stock, cover; stand about 5 minutes or until stock is absorbed, fluffing with fork occasionally. Transfer couscous to large bowl; stir in apricots, sultanas, onion and herbs.
2 Meanwhile, cook beef in heated oiled frying pan until cooked as desired. Cover beef; stand 5 minutes. Slice thinly.
3 Place nuts and seeds in small heated frying pan; cook, stirring, until fragrant and nuts are toasted. Place nut mixture in screw-top jar with dressing; shake well.
4 Serve beef on couscous mixture; drizzle with dressing.

on the table in 35 minutes
serves 4 **per serving** 13.5g total fat (4.9g saturated fat); 2834kJ (678 cal); 91.5g carbohydrate; 46.5g protein; 4.4g fibre

Beef and noodle salad

400g beef eye fillet steaks
2 tablespoons soy sauce
1 tablespoon sesame oil
250g bean thread noodles
1 medium red onion (170g), sliced thinly
1 large carrot (180g), sliced thinly
1 lebanese cucumber (130g), seeded, sliced thinly
½ cup loosely packed fresh coriander leaves
¼ cup coarsely chopped fresh thai basil
¼ cup (60ml) lime juice
¼ cup (60ml) sweet chilli sauce
2 tablespoons fish sauce

1 Combine beef with sauce and half of the oil in medium bowl.
2 Place noodles in large heatproof bowl, cover with boiling water, stand until just tender; drain. Rinse under cold water; drain.
3 Combine noodles in large bowl with onion, carrot, cucumber and herbs. Combine juice, sauces and remaining oil in small jug.
4 Drain beef; discard marinade. Cook beef in heated lightly oiled medium frying pan until browned both sides and cooked as desired. Cover; stand 10 minutes then slice thinly. Add beef and dressing to salad; toss gently to combine. Serve with lime wedges, if desired.

on the table in 25 minutes
serves 4 **per serving** 11.8g total fat (3.2g saturated fat); 1639kJ (392 cal); 42.2g carbohydrate; 26.9g protein; 3.6g fibre
tip bean thread noodles, also known as wun sen, glass or cellophane noodles, are made from mung beans. These delicate, fine noodles must be softened in boiling water before use; after soaking, they become transparent.

Curried pork stir-fry with wild rice

2 cups (400g) basmati rice
½ cup (90g) wild rice
800g pork fillets, sliced thinly
2 teaspoons vegetable oil
2 cloves garlic, crushed
1cm piece fresh ginger (5g), grated
1 teaspoon ground coriander
1 teaspoon ground cumin
1 teaspoon ground turmeric
2 teaspoons garam masala
500g brussels sprouts, halved
300g patty-pan squash, quartered
1 medium leek (350g), sliced thinly
¼ cup (60ml) lemon juice
¼ cup (60ml) water
200g low-fat yogurt
1 tablespoon finely chopped fresh mint
1 tablespoon finely chopped fresh coriander
½ cup (140g) low-fat yogurt, extra

1 Cook rices, in separate medium saucepans of boiling water, until each is just tender (wild rice will take longer to cook than basmati); drain. Combine rices in large bowl; cover to keep warm.
2 Meanwhile, heat wok; stir-fry pork, in batches, until browned all over.
3 Heat oil in wok; stir-fry garlic, ginger and spices until fragrant. Add sprouts, squash, leek, juice and the water; stir-fry until vegetables are just tender.
4 Return pork to wok with yogurt and herbs; stir-fry, tossing until combined.
5 Serve pork stir-fry with rice, topped with extra yogurt.

on the table in 30 minutes
serves 6 **per serving** 5.6g total fat (1.4g saturated fat); 2077kJ (497 cal); 64.2g carbohydrate; 42.9g protein; 6.3g fibre
tip you can replace the two individual rices in this recipe with one of the commercial blends of basmati and wild rice available in some supermarkets; cook a 500g package of the combined rices according to the manufacturer's instructions on the packet.

Moroccan lamb cutlets

24 french-trimmed lamb cutlets (960g)
1 teaspoon ground coriander
2 teaspoons ground cumin
2 teaspoons sweet paprika
¼ teaspoon cayenne pepper
1 clove garlic, crushed
1 tablespoon finely chopped fresh flat-leaf parsley
2 tablespoons olive oil
1 teaspoon cumin seeds, toasted
¼ cup (60g) prepared baba ghanoush

1 Combine lamb with ground coriander and cumin, paprika, cayenne
pepper, garlic, parsley and oil in medium bowl.
2 Cook lamb on heated oiled grill plate (or grill or barbecue) until cooked
as desired.
3 Sprinkle lamb with cumin seeds; serve with baba ghanoush.

on the table in 15 minutes
serves 6 **per serving** 14.8g total fat (4.7g saturated fat); 974kJ (233 cal);
0.5g carbohydrate; 24.5g protein; 1.1g fibre
tip prepared baba ghanoush can be purchased from some supermarkets
and delicatessens.

Sang choy bow

2 teaspoons sesame oil
500g lean pork mince
1 small brown onion (80g), chopped finely
1 clove garlic, crushed
1cm piece fresh ginger (5g), grated
2 tablespoons water
100g shiitake mushrooms, chopped finely
2 tablespoons soy sauce
2 tablespoons oyster sauce
1 tablespoon lime juice
2 cups (160g) bean sprouts
4 green onions, sliced thinly
¼ cup coarsely chopped fresh coriander
12 large butter lettuce leaves

1 Heat oil in wok; stir-fry pork, brown onion, garlic and ginger until pork is just changed in colour.
2 Add the water, mushrooms, sauces and juice; stir-fry until mushrooms are just tender. Remove from heat, add sprouts, green onion and coriander; toss gently to combine.
3 Divide lettuce leaves among serving plates; spoon pork mixture into leaves.

on the table in 30 minutes
serves 4 **per serving** 4.7g total fat (1.0g saturated fat); 849kJ (203 cal); 5.6g carbohydrate; 32.5g protein; 3.7g fibre

Marmalade-glazed pork cutlets

½ cup (125ml) dry red wine
⅓ cup (115g) orange marmalade
1 clove garlic, crushed
⅓ cup (80ml) fresh orange juice
1 tablespoon olive oil
4 lean pork cutlets (940g)

1 Combine wine, marmalade, garlic and juice in small saucepan; bring to a boil. Remove from heat.
2 Heat oil in large frying pan; cook pork until browned both sides and just cooked through, brushing occasionally with marmalade glaze. Serve with steamed rice and buk choy, if desired.

on the table in 25 minutes
serves 4 **per serving** 8.6g total fat (2.0g saturated fat); 1271kJ (304 cal); 20.1g carbohydrate; 30.4g protein; 0.4g fibre

Teriyaki lamb stir-fry

2 teaspoons olive oil
800g lean lamb strips
2 teaspoons sesame oil
2 cloves garlic, crushed
1 medium brown onion (150g), sliced thickly
1 fresh long red chilli, sliced thinly
⅓ cup (80ml) teriyaki sauce
¼ cup (60ml) sweet chilli sauce
500g baby buk choy, quartered
175g broccolini, chopped coarsely

1 Heat olive oil in wok; stir-fry lamb, in batches, until cooked as desired.
2 Heat sesame oil in wok; stir-fry garlic, onion and chilli until fragrant.
Add sauces; bring to a boil. Add buk choy and broccolini; stir-fry until
buk choy just wilts and broccolini is just tender. Return lamb to wok;
stir-fry until heated through.

on the table in 30 minutes
serves 4 **per serving** 12.6g total fat (3.9g saturated fat); 1463kJ
(350 cal); 7.2g carbohydrate; 49.1g protein; 4.9g fibre

Butterflied pork steaks with pear and apple salsa

1 tablespoon water
2 tablespoons lemon juice
2 teaspoons white sugar
1 medium green apple (150g), cut into 1cm pieces
1 medium red apple (150g), cut into 1cm pieces
1 small pear (180g), peeled, cut into 1cm pieces
1 long green chilli, chopped finely
1 tablespoon finely chopped fresh mint
8 x 100g butterflied pork steaks, trimmed

1 Combine the water, juice and sugar in medium bowl, stirring, until sugar dissolves. Add apples, pear, chilli and mint; toss gently to combine.
2 Cook pork on heated lightly oiled grill plate (or grill or barbecue) until browned both sides and cooked as desired. Serve pork with salsa.

on the table in 25 minutes
serves 4 **per serving** 3.3g total fat (1.0g saturated fat); 1137kJ (272 cal); 13.2g carbohydrate; 45.6g protein; 2.2g fibre

Lamb kofta with yogurt and chilli tomato sauces

1kg lean lamb mince
1 large brown onion (200g), chopped finely
1 clove garlic, crushed
1 tablespoon ground cumin
2 teaspoons ground turmeric
2 teaspoons ground allspice
1 tablespoon finely chopped fresh mint
2 tablespoons finely chopped fresh flat-leaf parsley
1 egg, beaten lightly
6 pocket pitta bread, quartered
yogurt sauce
200g low-fat yogurt
1 clove garlic, crushed
1 tablespoon finely chopped fresh flat-leaf parsley
chilli tomato sauce
¼ cup (60ml) tomato sauce
¼ cup (60ml) chilli sauce

1 Using hand, combine lamb, onion, garlic, spices, herbs and egg in large bowl; shape mixture into 18 balls.
2 Mould balls around skewers to form sausage shapes. Cook, in batches, on heated oiled grill plate (or grill or barbecue) until browned all over and cooked through.
3 Meanwhile, make yogurt sauce; make chilli tomato sauce.
4 Serve kofta with pitta and sauces.
yogurt sauce combine yogurt, garlic and parsley in small bowl.
chilli tomato sauce combine tomato and chilli sauces in small bowl.

on the table in 30 minutes
serves 6 **per serving** 8.2g total fat (3.1g saturated fat); 1547kJ (370 cal); 28.1g carbohydrate; 43.9g protein; 2.5g fibre
tip soak 18 bamboo skewers in water before use to prevent them scorching and splintering.

Veal cutlets with brussels sprouts and celeriac mash

2 large potatoes (600g), chopped coarsely
500g celeriac, chopped coarsely
1 cup (250ml) buttermilk, warmed
4 x 200g veal chops
300g brussels sprouts, halved
20g butter, melted
2 teaspoons finely chopped fresh thyme
2 tablespoons lemon juice

1 Boil, steam or microwave potato and celeriac, separately, until tender; drain. Mash together with buttermilk in large bowl until smooth. Cover to keep warm.
2 Meanwhile, cook veal on heated oiled grill plate (or grill or barbecue), uncovered, until cooked as desired.
3 Cook sprouts on heated oiled flat plate, uncovered, until browned. Combine sprouts in medium bowl with butter, thyme and juice. Serve veal with mash and sprouts.

on the table in 30 minutes
serves 4 **per serving** 8.9g total fat (4.4g saturated fat); 1530kJ (366 cal); 27.2g carbohydrate; 39.1g protein; 9.2g fibre

Hokkien noodle and pork stir-fry

600g hokkien noodles
1 tablespoon cornflour
½ cup (125ml) water
¼ cup (60ml) kecap manis
¼ cup (60ml) hoisin sauce
2 tablespoons rice vinegar
2 tablespoons peanut oil
600g pork fillet, sliced thinly
1 medium brown onion (150g), sliced thickly
2 cloves garlic, crushed
1cm piece fresh ginger (5g), grated
150g sugar snap peas, trimmed
1 medium red capsicum (200g), sliced thinly
1 medium yellow capsicum (200g), sliced thinly
200g baby buk choy, quartered

1 Place noodles in large heatproof bowl, cover with boiling water.
Separate noodles with fork; drain.
2 Blend cornflour with the water in small bowl; stir in sauces and vinegar.
3 Heat half of the oil in wok; stir-fry pork, in batches, until browned all over.
4 Heat remaining oil in wok; stir-fry onion, garlic and ginger until onion
softens. Add peas, capsicums and buk choy; stir-fry until vegetables are
just tender.
5 Return pork to wok with noodles and sauce mixture; stir-fry until sauce
thickens slightly.

on the table in 30 minutes
serves 4 **per serving** 14.3g total fat (3.0g saturated fat); 2232kJ
(534 cal); 53.3g carbohydrate; 43.5g protein; 7.6g fibre

Cajun lamb backstraps with four-bean salad

1 tablespoon cajun seasoning
800g lean lamb backstraps
1 small red onion (100g), chopped finely
2 small egg tomatoes (260g), chopped coarsely
60g baby spinach leaves, shredded finely
2 x 300g cans four-bean mix, rinsed, drained
¼ cup firmly packed fresh coriander leaves
¼ cup firmly packed fresh flat-leaf parsley
⅓ cup (80ml) bottled french dressing

1 Using hands, rub seasoning onto lamb; cook lamb on heated oiled grill plate (or grill or barbecue) until browned and cooked as desired. Cover; stand 5 minutes, slice thickly.
2 Meanwhile, place remaining ingredients in large bowl; toss gently to combine.
3 Serve salad topped with lamb.

on the table in 25 minutes
serves 4 **per serving** 12.6g total fat (3.9g saturated fat); 1718kJ (411 cal); 18.8g carbohydrate; 51.4g protein; 7.6g fibre

Veal and fettuccine in sage mustard sauce

500g fettuccine
8 x 80g veal steaks
2 cloves garlic, crushed
2 tablespoons wholegrain mustard
¾ cup (180ml) dry white wine
1 cup (250ml) chicken stock
2 teaspoons finely shredded fresh sage
300g snow peas, sliced thinly

1 Cook pasta in large saucepan of boiling water, uncovered, until just tender; drain.
2 Meanwhile, cook veal, in batches, in large lightly oiled frying pan until browned both sides and cooked as desired; cover to keep warm.
3 Add garlic and mustard to same pan; cook, stirring, 1 minute. Add wine and stock; bring to a boil. Reduce heat; simmer, uncovered, about 5 minutes or until liquid reduces by half. Stir in sage.
4 Boil, steam or microwave snow peas until just tender; drain.
5 Cut veal pieces in half on the diagonal. Combine pasta and snow peas; divide among serving plates. Top with veal pieces; drizzle with sage mustard sauce.

on the table in 25 minutes
serves 8 **per serving** 2.2g total fat (0.5g saturated fat); 1375kJ (329 cal); 44.8g carbohydrate; 26.5g protein; 3.1g fibre

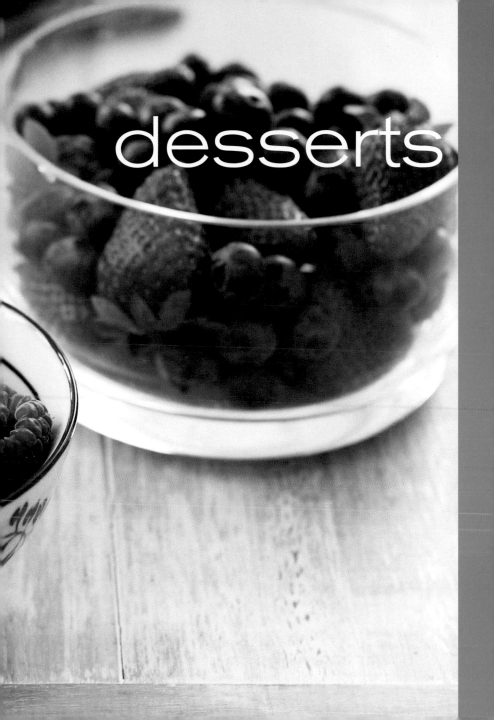

desserts

Grilled bananas with malibu syrup

4 large ripe bananas (920g)
⅓ cup (80ml) maple syrup
2 tablespoons Malibu
¼ cup (15g) toasted shredded coconut

1 Split bananas lengthways. Combine maple syrup and liqueur;
brush about a quarter of the mixture over the cut-sides of bananas.
2 Cook bananas, cut-side down, on heated lightly oiled grill plate
(or grill or barbecue) until lightly browned and heated through.
3 Serve bananas while hot, drizzled with warmed remaining syrup
and coconut.

on the table in 25 minutes
serves 4 **per serving** 2.7g total fat (2.2g saturated fat); 1191kJ (285 cal);
53.6g carbohydrate; 2.9g protein; 3.9g fibre
tip Malibu is the brand name of a rum-based coconut liqueur.

Grilled fruit kebabs with passionfruit sauce

½ cup (125ml) water
¼ cup (60ml) orange juice
½ cup (110g) caster sugar
1 tablespoon honey
½ cup (125ml) passionfruit pulp
2 tablespoons orange-flavoured liqueur
1 small pineapple (800g), chopped coarsely
1 small papaya (650g), chopped coarsely
2 large bananas (460g), sliced thickly
250g strawberries

1 Combine the water, juice, sugar and honey in small saucepan. Stir over heat, without boiling, until sugar dissolves; bring to a boil. Reduce heat, simmer, uncovered, without stirring, about 8 minutes or until mixture thickens slightly. Remove from heat; stir in passionfruit pulp and liqueur. Cool 5 minutes.
2 Meanwhile, thread fruit onto skewers; brush with passionfruit sauce. Cook kebabs on heated oiled grill plate (or grill or barbecue) until browned lightly, brushing occasionally with passionfruit sauce.
3 Serve kebabs drizzled with remaining passionfruit sauce.

on the table in 30 minutes
serves 4 **per serving** 0.5g total fat (0.0g saturated fat); 1559kJ (373 cal); 74.2g carbohydrate; 4.9g protein; 12.2g fibre
tips you will need about 6 passionfruit for this recipe. Soak eight bamboo skewers in water before use to prevent them scorching and splintering. We used Cointreau, but you can use triple-sec, Grand Marnier or any orange-flavoured liqueur you like; you can also omit alcohol completely.

Summer berry stack

450g loaf brioche bread
250g strawberries, sliced thickly
150g raspberries
150g blueberries
1 tablespoon icing sugar
blackberry coulis
300g frozen blackberries
¼ cup (40g) icing sugar
¼ cup (60ml) water

1 Make blackberry coulis.
2 Cut twelve 1cm-thick slices from bread; using 7cm cutter, cut one round from each slice.
3 Combine berries in medium bowl.
4 Place one round on each plate; divide a third of the berries among rounds. Place another round on top of each stack; divide half of the remaining berries among stacks. Place remaining rounds on berry stacks; top with remaining berries.
5 Pour coulis over stacks; dust each with sifted icing sugar.
blackberry coulis stir ingredients in medium saucepan over high heat; bring to a boil. Reduce heat; simmer, uncovered, 3 minutes. Strain coulis into medium jug; cool 10 minutes.

on the table in 25 minutes
serves 4 **per serving** 7.2g total fat (3g saturated fat); 1313kJ (314 cal); 55.3g carbohydrate; 7.5g protein; 9.7g fibre

Macerated fruits

1 cup (80g) dried apples
1 cup (140g) dried apricots
2 cups (500ml) apple juice
2 tablespoons lemon juice

1 Combine ingredients in small bowl.
2 Cover; refrigerate 30 minutes.

on the table in 35 minutes
serves 4 **per serving** 0.2g total fat (0.0g saturated fat); 723kJ (173 cal);
41.4g carbohydrate; 1.9g protein; 5g fibre
tip fruit can be macerated overnight.

Chocolate fudge cakes with coffee syrup

½ cup (50g) cocoa powder
1 cup (220g) firmly packed brown sugar
½ cup (125ml) boiling water
85g dark eating chocolate, chopped finely
2 egg yolks
¼ cup (30g) almond meal
⅓ cup (50g) wholemeal plain flour
4 egg whites
coffee syrup
¾ cup (165g) firmly packed brown sugar
¾ cup (180ml) water
1 tablespoon instant coffee powder

1 Preheat oven to 160°C/140°C fan-forced. Lightly grease 12-hole
(⅓-cup/80ml) muffin pan.
2 Combine sifted cocoa and sugar in large bowl; blend in the water then
chocolate, stir until smooth. Stir in egg yolks, almond meal and flour.
3 Beat egg whites in small bowl with electric mixer until soft peaks form.
Fold egg whites into chocolate mixture, in two batches; divide mixture
among prepared holes of muffin pan.
4 Bake, uncovered, about 20 minutes.
5 Meanwhile, make coffee syrup.
6 Stand cakes in pan 5 minutes. Divide cakes among plates; drizzle hot
cakes with hot coffee syrup.
coffee syrup stir sugar and the water in small saucepan over low heat
until sugar dissolves; bring to a boil. Reduce heat; simmer, uncovered,
without stirring, about 15 minutes or until syrup thickens. Stir in coffee;
strain into small heatproof jug.

on the table in 35 minutes
makes 12 **per cake** 5.1g total fat (2g saturated fat); 895kJ (214 cal);
39.5g carbohydrate; 4.2g protein; 1.2g fibre

Caramelised figs with spiced yogurt

1 cup (280g) low-fat yogurt
¼ cup (35g) toasted pistachios, chopped coarsely
¼ teaspoon ground nutmeg
1 tablespoon caster sugar
6 large fresh figs (480g)
1 tablespoon honey

1 Combine yogurt, nuts, nutmeg and sugar in small bowl.
2 Halve figs lengthways. Brush cut-side of figs with honey.
3 Cook figs, cut-side down, uncovered, in heated lightly oiled large frying pan 5 minutes. Turn figs; cook, uncovered, 5 minutes or until browned lightly. Serve figs with spiced yogurt.

on the table in 20 minutes
serves 4 **per serving** 6.0g total fat (1.3g saturated fat); 777kJ (186 cal); 26.1g carbohydrate; 6.8g protein; 3.6g fibre

Kiwi fruit, lychee and lime salad

8 kiwi fruits (680g), cut into wedges
16 fresh lychees (400g)
⅓ cup fresh mint leaves
⅓ cup (80ml) lime juice

1 Combine ingredients in small bowl.

on the table in 10 minutes
serves 4 **per serving** 0.5g total fat (0.0g saturated fat); 535kJ (128 cal); 26.8g carbohydrate; 3.2g protein; 6.1g fibre

Stewed prunes with orange

2 cups (340g) seeded dried prunes
1 cup (250ml) orange juice
1 cup (250ml) water
4 x 5cm strips orange rind, sliced thinly
2 cinnamon sticks
8 cardamon pods, bruised

1 Place ingredients in small saucepan; bring to a boil. Reduce heat, simmer, covered, 10 minutes.
2 Serve stewed prunes with low-fat yogurt, if desired.

on the table in 25 minutes
serves 4 **per serving** 0.4g total fat (0.0g saturated fat); 752kJ (180 cal); 42.2g carbohydrate; 2.3g protein; 6.8g fibre

Blood plums with honey and cardamon yogurt

1 cup (280g) low-fat yogurt
2 tablespoons honey
1 teaspoon ground cardamom
8 small blood plums (720g), quartered

1 Combine yogurt, honey and cardamom in small bowl.
2 Place plums on small serving plate; drizzle with yogurt mixture.

on the table in 10 minutes
serves 4   **per serving** 4.4g total fat (0.0g saturated fat); 732kJ (175 cal);
26.7g carbohydrate; 4.2g protein; 3.6g fibre

Panettone with ricotta and caramelised peaches

3 medium peaches (450g)
⅓ cup (75g) firmly packed brown sugar
2 teaspoons amaretto
2 x 100g panettone
1 cup (200g) low-fat ricotta cheese

1 Cut each peach into eight wedges. Cook peach and sugar in large lightly oiled frying pan about 5 minutes or until sugar dissolves. Reduce heat, simmer, uncovered, about 10 minutes or until peach is soft and pan juices are syrupy. Gently stir in liqueur.
2 Slice each panettone crossways into six pieces; toast panettone lightly both sides.
3 Divide panettone among serving plates; top with cheese and peach, drizzle with pan juices.

on the table in 25 minutes
serves 6 **per serving** 6.9g total fat (4.0g saturated fat); 953kJ (228 cal); 32.9g carbohydrate; 6.6g protein; 2.0g fibre
tips amaretto, originally from Italy, is an almond-flavoured liqueur and can be purchased from liquor stores. If small panettone are unavailable, cut 7cm rounds from large panettone, brioche or fruit bread.

Tropical fruit skewers with coconut dressing

2 medium bananas (400g)
½ medium pineapple (625g)
2 large starfruit (320g)
1 large mango (600g), chopped coarsely
coconut dressing
⅓ cup (80ml) coconut-flavoured liqueur
¼ cup (60ml) light coconut milk
1 tablespoon grated palm sugar
1cm piece fresh ginger (5g), grated finely

1 Make coconut dressing.
2 Cut each unpeeled banana into eight pieces. Cut unpeeled pineapple into eight slices; cut slices in half. Cut each starfruit into eight slices.
3 Make coconut dressing.
4 Thread fruit onto skewers, alternating varieties. Cook skewers on grill plate (or grill or barbecue), brushing with a little of the dressing, until browned lightly.
5 Serve skewers drizzled with remaining dressing.
coconut dressing place ingredients in screw-top jar; shake well.

on the table in 35 minutes
serves 4 **per serving** 3.7g total fat (2.7g saturated fat); 1321kJ (316 cal); 50.9g carbohydrate; 3.9g protein; 6.4g fibre
tips we used Malibu for the dressing, but you can use any coconut-flavoured liqueur. Soak eight bamboo skewers in water before use to prevent them from scorching and splintering.

Mixed berries with sponge fingers

12 savoiardi sponge finger biscuits (140g)
1 cup (250ml) cranberry juice
400g low-fat french vanilla frûche
150g fresh raspberries
150g fresh blueberries

1 Dip biscuits in juice; divide among four 1½-cup (375ml) serving glasses. Sprinkle remaining juice over biscuits.
2 Divide half of the frûche mixture among glasses; sprinkle with half of the berries. Repeat layering with remaining frûche and remaining berries.

on the table in 15 minutes
serves 4 **per serving** 2.1g total fat (0.7g saturated fat); 1095kJ (262 cal); 47.0g carbohydrate; 11.9g protein; 3.1g fibre

Apple and pear compote with dates

4 small apples (520g)
4 small pears (720g)
⅔ cup (180ml) lemon juice
1⅓ cup (220g) coarsely chopped dried dates
1 tablespoon finely grated orange rind
⅔ cup (180ml) orange juice

1 Peel and core apples and pears; cut into 2cm pieces. Combine apple and pear in small saucepan with lemon juice; cook, covered, over low heat, about 10 minutes or until fruit softens.
2 Meanwhile, combine dates, rind and orange juice in small saucepan; cook, uncovered, over low heat, stirring occasionally, about 5 minutes or until liquid is absorbed.
3 Serve fruit compote, warm or cold, topped with date mixture and finely shredded orange rind, if desired.

on the table in 30 minutes
serves 4 **per serving** 0.5g total fat (0.0g saturated fat); 1242kJ (297 cal); 72.1g carbohydrate; 2.4g protein; 9.9g fibre

Peach galette

1 sheet ready-rolled puff pastry with canola, thawed
3 medium peaches (450g)
1 tablespoon brown sugar
1 tablespoon plum jam, warmed, strained

1 Preheat oven to 220°C/200°C fan-forced. Grease oven tray.
2 Place pastry sheet on tray.
3 Place unpeeled peaches in large heatproof bowl; cover with boiling water. Stand about 1 minute or until skins can be slipped off easily. Slice peaches thinly; discard seeds.
4 Arrange peach slices on pastry, leaving 2cm border around edge; fold over edges of pastry. Sprinkle sugar evenly over peach galette.
5 Bake, uncovered, about 15 minutes or until pastry is browned lightly. Brush hot galette with jam. Serve dusted with sifted icing sugar, if desired.

on the table in 25 minutes
serves 6 **per serving** 6.4g total fat (0.5g saturated fat); 589kJ (141 cal); 18.2g carbohydrate; 2.1g protein; 1.3g fibre
tips a galette is a French flaky pastry tart that can be either savoury or sweet, and makes a popular summer dessert. Any of the season's stone fruits, such as plums or nectarines, can be substituted for the peaches.

Passionfruit soufflés

1 tablespoon caster sugar
2 egg yolks
⅓ cup (80ml) fresh passionfruit pulp
2 tablespoons orange-flavoured liqueur
½ cup (80g) icing sugar
4 egg whites
2 teaspoons icing sugar, extra

1 Preheat oven to 180°C/160°C fan-forced. Grease four 1 cup (250ml) ovenproof dishes. Sprinkle insides of dishes evenly with caster sugar; shake away excess. Place dishes on oven tray.
2 Whisk yolks, passionfruit pulp, liqueur and 2 tablespoons of the icing sugar in large bowl until mixture is combined.
3 Beat egg whites in small bowl with electric mixer until soft peaks form. Gradually add remaining icing sugar; beat until firm peaks form.
4 Gently fold egg-white mixture, in two batches, into passionfruit mixture; divide mixture among dishes.
5 Bake, uncovered, about 12 minutes or until soufflés are puffed and browned lightly. Dust tops with extra sifted icing sugar.

on the table in 25 minutes
serves 4 **per serving** 2.9g total fat (0.9g saturated fat); 869kJ (208 cal); 31.9g carbohydrate; 5.8g protein; 2.8g fibre
tips you need 4 large passionfruit for this recipe.
We used Cointreau in our soufflés, but you can use triple-sec, Grand Marnier or any orange-flavoured liqueur you like.

Blueberry and fillo pastry stacks

4 sheets fillo pastry
cooking-oil spray
125g packaged light cream cheese
½ cup (125ml) light cream
2 teaspoons finely grated orange rind
2 tablespoons icing sugar
blueberry sauce
300g blueberries
¼ cup (55g) caster sugar
2 tablespoons orange juice
1 teaspoon cornflour

1 Preheat oven to 200°C/180°C fan-forced. Grease oven trays.
2 Spray one fillo sheet with oil; layer with another fillo sheet. Halve
fillo stack lengthways; cut each half into thirds to form six fillo squares.
Repeat process with remaining fillo sheets.
3 Place 12 fillo squares onto trays; spray with oil. Bake, uncovered, about
5 minutes or until browned lightly; cool 10 minutes.
4 Meanwhile, make blueberry sauce.
5 Beat cheese, cream, rind and half of the sugar in small bowl with
electric mixer until smooth.
6 Place one fillo square on each serving plate; spoon half of the cheese
mixture and half of the blueberry sauce over squares. Repeat layering
process, finishing with fillo squares; dust with remaining sifted sugar.
blueberry sauce cook blueberries, sugar and half of the juice in small
saucepan, stirring, until sugar dissolves. Stir in blended cornflour and
remaining juice; cook, stirring, until mixture boils and thickens slightly.
Remove from heat; cool 10 minutes.

on the table in 25 minutes
serves 4 **per serving** 12.9g total fat (7.9g saturated fat); 1304kJ (312 cal);
42.0g carbohydrate; 6.0g protein; 1.9g fibre

Papaya with passionfruit and lime

3 small papaya (2kg), cut into thick wedges
⅓ cup (80ml) passionfruit pulp
2 tablespoons lime juice

1 Place papaya on medium serving plate.
2 Drizzle with passionfruit and juice.

on the table in 20 minutes
serves 4 **per serving** 0.4g total fat (0.0g saturated fat); 560kJ (134 cal);
25.1g carbohydrate; 2.1g protein; 10.7g fibre
tips we used the red-fleshed hawaiian or fijian variety instead of the
yellow-fleshed papaya here. You will need 1 passionfruit for this recipe.

Minty chocolate mousse

150g dark eating chocolate, melted
4 eggs, separated
2 tablespoons crème de menthe
1 tablespoon caster sugar

1 Combine chocolate, egg yolks and liqueur in large bowl.
2 Beat egg whites and sugar in small bowl with electric mixer until soft peaks form. Fold into chocolate mixture in two batches.
3 Divide mousse mixture among six ¾-cup (180ml) glasses, cover; refrigerate about 15 minutes or until set. Serve with fresh raspberries, if desired.

on the table in 35 minutes
serves 6 **per serving** 11.1g total fat (8.0g saturated fat); 928kJ (222 cal); 20.6g carbohydrate; 5.4g protein; 1.2g fibre
tip you can replace the crème de menthe with any liqueur of your choice or, if making for children, use lime cordial (concentrate) instead.

Crushed pavlovas with honey yogurt and mixed berries

250g strawberries, halved
150g blueberries
120g raspberries
10 mini pavlova shells (100g)
1kg honey low-fat yogurt

1 Combine berries in medium bowl. Crush pavlovas coarsely into small bowl.
2 Divide yogurt among serving bowls; sprinkle with berries and crushed pavlova.

on the table in 15 minutes
serves 6 **per serving** 0.7g total fat (0.3g saturated fat); 878kJ (210 cal); 37.7g carbohydrate; 11.4g protein; 2.4g fibre
tips use any combination of your favourite berries in this recipe; if fresh ones are unavailable, you can use thawed frozen berries. This recipe should be made just before serving. We used mini pavlova shells here, but a single large pavlova shell can be used instead.

glossary

allspice also known as pimento or jamaican pepper.

bacon rashers also known as bacon slices; made from cured and smoked pork side.

bean sprouts also known as bean shoots; tender new growths of assorted beans and seeds germinated for consumption as sprouts.

beetroot also known as red beets; firm, round root vegetable.

bicarbonate of soda also called baking soda; used as a leavening agent in baking.

broccolini a cross between broccoli and Chinese kale. Looks like broccoli but is milder and sweeter in taste.

buk choy also known as bok choy, pak choi, chinese white cabbage or chinese chard; has a fresh, mild mustard taste. Use both stems and leaves. Baby buk choy, also known as pak kat farang or shanghai bok choy, is much smaller and more tender than buk choy. Its mildly acrid, distinctively appealing taste makes it one of the most commonly used asian greens.

butter we use salted butter unless stated otherwise; 125g is equal to 1 stick (4 ounces) in other recipes.

capsicum also known as pepper or bell pepper.

celeriac tuberous root with knobbly brown skin, white flesh and a celery-like flavour. Keep peeled celeriac in acidulated water to keep it from discolouring.

char siu sauce also called chinese barbecue sauce; a paste-like ingredient that is dark-red-brown in colour, with a sharp sweet and spicy flavour. Made with fermented soybeans, honey and various spices, char siu can be diluted and used as a marinade or brushed directly onto grilling meat.

cheese

cheddar most common cow-milk tasty cheese; should be aged, hard and have a pronounced bite. We use a version having no more than 20 per cent fat when calling for low-fat cheese.

cottage fresh, white, unripened curd cheese with a lumpy consistency and mild, sweet flavour. Fat content ranges between 15 to 55 per cent, depending on whether it's made from whole, low-fat or fat-free cow milk.

cream cheese often called philadelphia or philly; a soft cow-milk cheese with a fat content ranging from 14 per cent to 33 per cent.

fetta Greek in origin; a crumbly textured goat- or sheep-milk cheese having a sharp, salty taste. Ripened and stored in salted whey; particularly good cubed and tossed into salads. We use a version having no more than 15 per cent fat when calling for low-fat cheese.

haloumi a Greek Cypriot cheese having a semi-firm, spongy texture and very salty yet sweet flavour. Ripened and stored in salted whey; it's best grilled or fried, and holds its shape well on being heated. Should be eaten while still warm as it becomes tough and rubbery on cooling.

mozzarella soft, spun-curd cheese; originating in southern Italy, it was traditionally made from water-buffalo milk. Now generally made from cow milk, it is the most popular pizza cheese due to its low melting point and elasticity when heated (used for texture rather than flavour). We use a version having no more than 17.5 per cent fat when calling for low-fat cheese.

parmesan also called parmigiano, parmesan is a hard, grainy cow-milk cheese originating in the Parma region of Italy. The curd is salted in brine for a month before being aged for up to 2 years, preferably in humid conditions.

pecorino Italian generic name for sheep-milk cheeses. This family of hard, white to pale-yellow cheeses, traditionally made in the Italian winter and spring when sheep graze on natural pastures, have been matured for 8 to 12 months. They are classified according to the area in which they were produced — romano from Rome, sardo from Sardinia, siciliano from Sicily and toscano from Tuscany. If you can't find it, use parmesan.

ricotta a soft, sweet, moist, white cow-milk cheese with a low fat content (about 8.5 per cent) and a slightly grainy texture. It roughly translates as "cooked again" and refers to ricotta's manufacture from a whey that is itself a by-product of other cheese making.

cocoa powder also called unsweetened cocoa; cocoa beans (cacao seeds) that have been fermented, roasted, shelled, ground into powder then cleared of most of the fat content. Unsweetened cocoa is used in hot chocolate drink mixtures; milk powder and sugar are added to the ground product.

coconut

milk not the liquid found inside the fruit (called coconut water), but the diluted liquid from the second pressing of the white flesh of a mature coconut (the first pressing produces coconut cream). Available in cans and cartons at most supermarkets.

shredded unsweetened thin strips of dried coconut flesh.

coriander also known as cilantro, pak chee or chinese parsley; bright-green-leafed herb having both pungent aroma and taste. Coriander seeds are dried and sold either whole or ground, and neither form tastes remotely like the fresh leaf but rather like an acrid combination of sage and caraway.

cornflour also called cornstarch. Available made from corn or wheat (wheaten cornflour, gluten-free, gives a lighter texture in cakes); used as a thickening agent.

couscous a fine, grain-like cereal product made from semolina; from the countries of North Africa. A semolina flour and water dough is sieved then dehydrated to produce minuscule even-sized pellets of couscous; it is

rehydrated by steaming or by adding warm liquid, and swells to three or four times its original size.

cumin seeds also called zeera or comino.

currants dried tiny, almost black raisins so-named from the grape type native to Corinth, Greece. These are not the same as fresh currants, which are the fruit of a plant in the gooseberry family.

daikon also called white radish; an everyday fixture at the Japanese table, this long, white horseradish has a wonderful, sweet flavour. After peeling, eat it raw in salads or shredded as a garnish; also great when sliced or cubed and cooked in stir-fries and casseroles. The flesh is white but the skin can be either white or black; buy those that are firm and unwrinkled from Asian food shops.

eggplant also known as aubergine.

fish sauce called naam pla on the label if Thai-made, nuoc naam if Vietnamese; the two are almost identical. Made from pulverised salted fermented fish (most often anchovies); has a pungent smell and strong taste. Available in varying degrees of intensity, so use according to your taste.

flour

plain also known as all-purpose; unbleached wheat flour is the best for baking: the gluten content ensures a strong dough, which produces a light result. Also used as a thickening agent in sauces and gravies.

wholemeal self-raising also called wholewheat self-raising flour; milled with the wheat germ so is higher in fibre and more nutritional than white flour. All-purpose plain wholemeal flour with baking powder and salt added; can be made at home with plain or wholemeal flour sifted with baking powder in the proportion of 1 cup flour to 2 teaspoons baking powder.

gai lan also known as gai larn, chinese broccoli and chinese kale; green vegetable appreciated more for its stems than its coarse leaves. Can be served steamed and stir-fried, in soups and noodle dishes.

garam masala literally meaning blended spices in its northern Indian place of origin; based on varying proportions of cardamom, cinnamon, cloves, coriander, fennel and cumin, roasted and ground together. Black pepper and chilli can be added for a hotter version.

ginger

fresh also known as green or root ginger; thick gnarled root of a tropical plant.

pickled pink or red in colour; found packaged in Asian food shops. Pickled paper-thin shavings of ginger in a mixture of vinegar, sugar and natural colouring. Mostly used in Japanese cooking.

gow gee wrappers wonton wrappers or spring roll pastry sheets, made of flour, egg and water; found in the refrigerated or freezer section of Asian food shops and many supermarkets. These come in different thicknesses and shapes. Thin wrappers work best in soups, while the thicker ones are best for frying; and the choice of round or square, small or large is dependent on the recipe.

harissa a North African paste made from dried red chillies, garlic, olive oil and caraway seeds; can be used as a rub for meat, an ingredient in sauces and dressings, or eaten on its own as a condiment. It is available ready-made from Middle Eastern food shops and some supermarkets.

hoisin sauce a thick, sweet and spicy Chinese barbecue sauce made from salted fermented soybeans, onions and garlic; used as a marinade or baste, or to accent stir-fries and barbecued or roasted foods. From Asian food shops and supermarkets.

kaffir lime leaves also called bai magrood, look like they are two glossy dark green leaves joined end to end, forming a rounded hourglass shape. Used fresh or dried in many South East Asian dishes, they are used like bay leaves or curry leaves, especially in Thai cooking. Sold fresh, dried or frozen, the dried leaves are less potent so double the number if using them as a substitute for fresh; a strip of fresh lime peel may be substituted for each kaffir lime leaf.

kecap manis a dark, thick sweet soy sauce used in most South East Asian cuisines. Depending on the manufacturer, the sauces's sweetness is derived from the addition of either molasses or palm sugar when brewed. Use as a condiment, dipping sauce, ingredient or marinade.

kumara the polynesian name of an orange-fleshed sweet potato often confused with yam.

lemon grass also called takrai, serai or

serah. A tall, clumping, lemon-smelling and tasting, sharp-edged aromatic tropical grass; the white lower part of the stem is used, finely chopped, in much of the cooking of South East Asia. Can be found, fresh, dried, powdered and frozen, in supermarkets and greengrocers as well as Asian food shops.

mesclun pronounced mess-kluhn; also called mixed greens or spring salad mix. A blend of assorted young lettuce and other green leaves.

minced meat also called ground meat, as in beef, pork, lamb and veal.

mirin a Japanese champagne-coloured cooking wine, made of glutinous rice and alcohol. It is used expressly for cooking and should not be confused with sake. A seasoned sweet mirin, manjo mirin, made of water, rice, corn syrup and alcohol, is used in various Japanese dipping sauces.

noodles

crispy fried crispy egg noodles that have been deep-fried then packaged for sale on supermarket shelves.

dried rice stick made from rice flour and water, available flat and wide or very thin

(vermicelli). Must be soaked in boiling water to soften.

fresh rice also called ho fun, khao pun, sen yau, pho or kway tiau, depending on the country of manufacture. Can be purchased in strands of various widths or large sheets weighing about 500g which are to be cut into the desired noodle size. Chewy and pure white, they do not need pre-cooking before use.

hokkien also called stir-fry noodles; fresh wheat noodles resembling thick, yellow-brown spaghetti needing no pre-cooking before use.

rice vermicelli also called sen mee, mei fun or bee hoon. Similar to bean thread noodles, only longer and made with rice flour instead of mung bean starch. Before using, soak dried noodles in hot water until softened; boil briefly then rinse with hot water.

soba thin, pale-brown noodle originally from Japan; made from buckwheat and varying proportions of wheat flour. Available dried and fresh, and in flavoured (for instance, green tea) varieties; eaten in soups, stir-fries and, chilled, on their own.

udon available fresh and dried, these broad, white, wheat Japanese

noodles are similar to the ones in home-made chicken noodle soup.

oil

cooking-oil spray we use a cholesterol-free cooking spray made from canola oil.

olive made from ripened olives. Extra virgin and virgin are the first and second press, respectively, and are therefore considered the best; the 'extra light' or 'light' name on other types refers to taste not fat levels.

peanut pressed from ground peanuts; the most commonly used oil in Asian cooking because of its high smoke point (capacity to handle high heat without burning).

sesame made from roasted, crushed, white sesame seeds; a flavouring rather than a cooking medium.

onion

green also known as scallion or (incorrectly) shallot; an immature onion picked before the bulb has formed, having a long, bright-green edible stalk.

red also called spanish, red spanish or bermuda onion; a sweet-flavoured, large, purple-red onion.

oyster sauce Asian in origin, this thick, richly flavoured brown sauce is made from oysters and their brine, cooked with salt and soy sauce, and thickened with starches. Use as a condiment.

pancetta an Italian unsmoked bacon, pork belly cured in salt and spices then rolled into a sausage shape and dried for several weeks.

patty-pan squash also called crookneck or custard marrow pumpkins; a round, slightly flat summer squash being yellow to pale green in colour and having a scalloped edge. Harvested young, it has firm white flesh and a distinct flavour.

prawns also known as shrimp.

prosciutto a kind of unsmoked Italian ham; salted, air-cured and aged, it is usually eaten uncooked.

rice paper sheets also called banh trang, made from rice flour and water then stamped into rounds; is quite brittle and breaks easily Dipped briefly in water, they become pliable wrappers for food.

rocket also called arugula, rugula and rucola; peppery green leaf eaten raw in salads or used in cooking. Baby rocket leaves are smaller and less peppery.

saffron stigma of a member of the crocus family, available ground or in strands; imparts a yellow-orange colour to food once infused. The quality can vary greatly; the best is the world's most expensive spice.

sake Japan's favourite wine, made from fermented rice; used for marinating, cooking and in dipping sauces. Substitute with dry sherry, vermouth or brandy if unavailable.

sambal oelek also called ulek or olek; a salty paste, Indonesian in origin, made from ground chillies and vinegar.

seaweed, yaki-nori dried seaweed used in Japanese cooking as a flavouring, garnish or for sushi. Sold in thin sheets, plain or toasted.

shallot also called french shallots, golden shallots or eschalots. Small, elongated, brown-skinned members of the onion family; they grow in tight clusters similar to garlic.

soy sauce also known as sieu; made from fermented soybeans. Several variaties are available in supermarkets and Asian food stores. We use Japanese soy sauce unless indicated otherwise.

japanese all-purpose low-sodium soy sauce made with more wheat content than its Chinese counterparts; fermented in barrels and aged.

light fairly thin in consistency and, while paler than the others, is the saltiest; used in dishes in which the natural colour of the ingredients is to be maintained. Not to be confused with salt-reduced or low-sodium soy sauces.

spinach also called english spinach and incorrectly, silverbeet.

sponge finger biscuits also called savoiardi or savoy biscuits, lady's fingers or sponge fingers, they are Italian-style crisp fingers made from sponge cake mixture.

star anise a dried star-shaped pod whose seeds have an astringent aniseed flavour; commonly used to flavour stocks and marinades.

sugar

brown an extremely soft, fine granulated sugar retaining molasses for its characteristic colour and flavour.

caster also known as superfine or finely granulated table sugar. The fine crystals dissolve easily so it is perfect for cakes, meringues and desserts.

icing also known as confectioners' sugar or powdered sugar.

palm also called nam tan pip, jaggery, jawa or gula melaka; made from the sap of the sugar palm tree. Light brown to black in colour and usually sold in rock-hard cakes; substitute with brown sugar if unavailable.

white also known as crystal sugar.

sumac a purple-red, astringent spice ground from berries growing on shrubs that flourish wild around the Mediterranean; adds a tart, lemony flavour to dips and dressings and goes well with barbecued meat. Can be found in Middle Eastern food stores.

sun-dried tomatoes tomato pieces that have been dried with salt; this dehydrates the tomato and concentrates the flavour. We use sun-dried tomatoes packaged in oil, unless otherwise specified.

tahini sesame seed paste available from Middle Eastern food stores; most often used in hummus and baba ghanoush.

tamari a thick, dark sauce made mainly from soy beans. Has a distinctive mellow flavour. Is used mainly as a dipping sauce or for basting. Available from most supermarkets and Asian food stores.

tamarind the tamarind tree produces clusters of hairy brown pods, each filled with seeds and a viscous pulp, that are dried and pressed into blocks of tamarind found in Asian food shops. Adds a sweet-sour, slightly astringent taste to marinades, pastes, sauces and dressings.

tat soi also called pak choy, rosette and chinese flat cabbage; a member of the same family as buk choy, it has the same mild flavour.

teriyaki sauce either home-made or commercially bottled, this Japanese sauce, made from soy sauce, mirin, sugar, ginger and other spices, imparts a distinctive glaze when brushed over grilled meat or poultry.

tofu, silken not a type of tofu but a reference to the process of straining soybean liquid through silk, this denotes best quality.

vanilla bean dried, long, thin pod from a tropical golden orchid grown in central and South America and Tahiti; the minuscule black seeds inside the bean are used to impart a vanilla flavour in baking and desserts. Place a whole bean in a jar of sugar to make the vanilla sugar often called for in recipes; a

bean can be used three or four times before losing its flavour.

vanilla extract obtained from vanilla beans infused in water; a non-alcoholic version of essence.

wasabi an Asian horseradish used to make the pungent, green-coloured sauce traditionally served with Japanese raw fish dishes; sold in powdered or paste form.

water chestnuts resemble true chestnuts in appearance, hence the English name. Small brown tubers with a crisp, white, nutty-tasting flesh. Their crunchy texture is best tasted fresh; canned water chestnuts are more easily obtained and can be kept for about a month in the fridge, once opened. Used, rinsed and drained, in salads and stir-fries.

worcestershire sauce thin, dark-brown spicy sauce developed by the British when in India; used as a seasoning for meat, gravies and cocktails, and as a condiment.

wombok also called chinese cabbage, peking or napa cabbage; elongated in shape with pale green, crinkly leaves.

zucchini also called courgette; its flowers are edible.

index

A

apple
  and celery juice 87
  and pear compote with
    dates 374
  and pear juice 64
  butterflied pork steaks
    with pear and apple
    salsa 337
  peach, apple and
    strawberry juice 44
  silverbeet, apple and
    celery juice 83
artichoke risotto 203
asian crispy noodle salad
  160
asian-flavoured trout with
  shiitake mushrooms 264
asian greens, chilli-chicken
  stir-fry with 299
asian greens, stir-fried, with
  mixed mushrooms 195
asparagus
  grilled asparagus
    with warm tomato
    dressing 184
  lemon grass and
    asparagus chicken 303
  poached eggs and
    asparagus with dill
    sauce 131
  prawn, scallop and
    asparagus salad with
    ginger dressing 252

B

bacon/ham
  breakfast with the lot 20
  egg-white omelette 39
  poached eggs with
    bacon, spinach and
    pecorino 28
balmain bugs and citrus
  salad 275
banana
  bruschetta with
    strawberry, banana
    and ricotta 36
  grilled bananas with
    malibu syrup 350
  soy smoothie 92
beans
  cajun lamb backstraps
    with four-bean salad 345
  crisp-skinned snapper
    with stir-fried vegetables
    and black beans 260

(*beans* continued)
  mexican bean salad
    with tortilla chips 183
  mixed bean salad 175
  potato and bean salad
    with lemon yogurt
    dressing 168
  tuna and white bean
    salad 148
  white bean salad 164
beef
  and noodle salad 325
  with green papaya, chilli
    and coriander salad 152
  meatball pho 108
  moroccan beef salad 322
beetroot, carrot and spinach
  juice 60
beetroot and celery juice,
  watercress 55
berries, mixed, with sponge
  fingers 373
blood plums with honey and
  cardamon yogurt 366
blue-eye, grilled, with
  gai lan 267
blueberry
  and fillo pastry stacks 381
  crushed pavlovas with
    honey yogurt and
    mixed berries 386
  mixed berries with
    sponge fingers 373
  mixed berry juice 47
  porridge with poached
    pears and blueberries 12
  strawberry hotcakes with
    blueberry sauce 16
  summer berry stack 354
breakfast with the lot 20
bream
  citrus-ginger steamed
    bream 220
  steamed asian bream 239
bruschetta with smoked
  salmon, cream cheese
  and rocket 32
bruschetta with strawberry,
  banana and ricotta 36
buk choy
  chicken with buk choy
    and flat mushrooms 311
  chilli rice noodles with
    buk choy 318
  garlic prawns and buk choy
    with herbed rice 123

(*buk choy* continued)
  prawn tamarind stir-fry
    with buk choy 279
  seared ocean trout with
    buk choy 272

C

caesar salad 144
cajun lamb backstraps with
  four-bean salad 345
calamari teppanyaki 224
carrot
  beetroot, carrot and
    spinach juice 60
  ginger and silverbeet
    juice 59
  orange, carrot and
    celery juice 67
  orange, carrot and
    ginger juice 96
celery
  apple and celery juice 87
  orange, carrot and
    celery juice 67
  silverbeet, apple and
    celery juice 83
  watercress, beetroot
    and celery juice 55
cheese *see also* ricotta
  bruschetta with smoked
    salmon, cream cheese
    and rocket 32
  egg-white omelette 39
  eggs, poached, with
    bacon, spinach and
    pecorino 28
  lemon-fetta couscous
    with steamed
    vegetables 208
  pan-fried haloumi with
    green salad 119
  spinach and cheese
    quesadillas 136
chicken
  and crunchy noodle
    salad 147
  and mixed pea stir-fry 296
  and tamarind stir-fry 307
  char-grilled chicken with
    warm tomato salad 308
  chilli-chicken stir-fry with
    asian greens 299
  curried chicken and
    zucchini soup 107
  glazed-chicken tortilla
    with sprout and herb
    salad 292

(*chicken* continued)
gourmet chicken
sandwiches 120
harissa chicken with
couscous salad 300
kebabs with papaya
salsa 284
lemon and artichoke
skewers 304
lemon grass and
asparagus chicken 303
pho 103
shredded chicken salad
291
skewers with chilli and
lime sauce 315
smoked chicken salad 188
tandoori pockets with
raita 127
tenderloin in green
peppercorn and
tarragon dressing 295
thai chicken and rice 287
thai chicken salad 155
vegetable and rice
noodle stir-fry 288
vietnamese chicken
salad 140
with buk choy and flat
mushrooms 311
with cucumber and
tomato salsa 312
chickpeas
felafel burgers 135
warm rice and chickpea
salad 171
chilli-chicken stir-fry with
asian greens 299
chilli rice noodles with
buk choy 318
chocolate fudge cakes
with coffee syrup 358
chocolate mousse,
minty 385
citrus compote 23
citrus-ginger steamed
bream 220
couscous salad, harissa
chicken with 300
couscous, lemon-fetta,
with steamed vegetables
208
curried pork stir-fry with
wild rice 326
D
duck, peking, rolls 128

E
eggplant with salsa fresca
196
eggs
breakfast with the lot 20
egg-white omelette 39
japanese omelette
salad 159
light-white frittata 124
pancetta, and 40
poached eggs and
asparagus with dill
sauce 131
poached eggs with
bacon, spinach and
pecorino 28
salade niçoise 179
scrambled eggs with dill
and smoked salmon 35
F
felafel burgers 135
figs, caramelised, with
spiced yogurt 361
fish *see* seafood
flathead, poached, with
herb salad 216
frittata, light-white 124
fruit kebabs, grilled, with
passionfruit sauce 353
fruits, macerated 357
G
galette, peach 377
garlic prawns and buk choy
with herbed rice 123
ginger
carrot, ginger and silver
beet juice 59
citrus-ginger steamed
bream 220
orange and ginger juice
51
orange and pineapple
juice 76
orange, carrot and
ginger juice 96
pear and ginger juice 79
pineapple, ginger and
mint juice 63
prawn, scallop and
asparagus salad with
ginger dressing 252
soba salad with
seaweed, ginger and
vegetables 187
tangelo and ginger juice
52

(*ginger* continued)
vegetable and soba
soup 111
grapefruit and blood orange
juice 48
grapefruit juice, mango
and 68
H
haloumi, pan-fried, with
green salad 119
harissa chicken with
couscous salad 300
hokkien noodle and pork
stir-fry 342
hotcakes, strawberry, with
blueberry sauce 16
J
japanese omelette salad
159
japanese-style tuna with
red-maple radish 219
K
kiwi fruit and green grape
juice 91
kiwi fruit, lychee and lime
salad 362
L
lamb
cajun lamb backstraps
with four-bean salad
345
chilli rice noodles with
buk choy 318
kofta with yogurt and chilli
tomato sauces 338
moroccan lamb cutlets
329
teriyaki lamb stir-fry 334
lavash wrap 116
leek and potato soup 104
lemon-fetta couscous
with steamed vegetables
208
lemon grass and asparagus
chicken 303
M
macerated fruits 357
mandarin juice 71
mango
and avocado salsa 24
and grapefruit juice 68
barbecued chilli prawns
with fresh mango
salad 263
orange, mango and
strawberry juice 88

marmalade-glazed pork
cutlets 333
meatball pho 108
mexican bean salad with
tortilla chips 183
morning trifles 27
moroccan beef salad 322
moroccan lamb cutlets 329
mousse, minty chocolate
385
muesli, untoasted 31
mulled-wine pork and
stone fruits 321
mushroom
asian-flavoured trout
with shiitake mushrooms
264
chicken with buk choy
and flat mushrooms
311
egg-white omelette 39
sautéed, on toast 19
stir-fried asian greens
with mixed mushrooms
195
mussels, steamed, with
saffron, chilli and
coriander 228

N
nasi goreng 192
noodles
asian crispy noodle
salad 160
beef and noodle salad
325
chicken and crunchy
noodle salad 147
chicken, vegetable and
rice noodle stir-fry 288
chilli rice noodles with
buk choy 318
ginger vegetable and
soba soup 111
hokkien noodle and
pork stir-fry 342
prawn, lime and rice
noodle stir-fry 256
seared tuna with
chilled soba 251
singapore noodles 200
soba and daikon salad
156
soba salad with
seaweed, ginger and
vegetables 187
vegetarian sukiyaki 211

O
ocean trout
oven-steamed ocean
trout 243
seared ocean trout with
buk choy 272
octopus, stir-fried, with
basil 240
omelette, egg-white 39
orange
and ginger juice 51
carrot and celery juice 67
carrot and ginger juice 96
ginger, orange and
pineapple juice 76
grapefruit and blood
orange juice 48
mango and strawberry
juice 88
pineapple, orange and
strawberry juice 75
stewed prunes with
orange 365

P
pancetta and eggs 40
panettone with ricotta
and caramelised
peaches 369
panzanella 167
papaya
beef with green papaya,
chilli and coriander
salad 152
chicken kebabs with
papaya salsa 284
pickled green papaya
salad 172
strawberry and papaya
juice 84
with passionfruit and
lime 382
passionfruit
grilled fruit kebabs
with passionfruit
sauce 353
papaya with passionfruit
and lime 382
soufflés 378
pasta primavera 199
pavlovas, crushed, with
honey yogurt and mixed
berries 386
peach
apple and strawberry
juice 44
galette 377

(*peach* continued)
panettone with ricotta
and caramelised
peaches 369
raspberry and peach
juice 80
pear
and ginger juice 79
and grape juice 72
apple and pear compote
with dates 374
apple and pear juice 64
butterflied pork steaks
with pear and apple
salsa 337
porridge with poached
pears and blueberries 12
pearl barley salad 180
peking duck rolls 128
pickled green papaya
salad 172
pineapple
ginger, orange and
pineapple juice 76
ginger and mint juice 63
orange and strawberry
juice 75
stir-fried prawns with
pineapple and chilli
salad 231
plums, blood, with honey
and cardamon yogurt 366
pork
butterflied pork steaks
with pear and apple
salsa 337
curried pork stir-fry with
wild rice 326
hokkien noodle and
pork stir-fry 342
marmalade-glazed pork
cutlets 333
mulled-wine pork and
stone fruits 321
sang choy bow 330
thai pork salad with kaffir
lime dressing 143
porridge with poached
pears and blueberries 12
potato and bean salad with
lemon yogurt dressing
168
prawn
barbecued chilli prawns
with fresh mango
salad 263

(*prawn* continued)
garlic prawns and buk
choy with herbed rice
123
grilled prawns with
tropical fruits 235
lime and rice noodle
stir-fry 256
microwave prawn and
pea risotto 244
tamarind stir-fry with
buk choy 279
scallop and asparagus
salad with ginger
dressing 252
steamed sweet chilli
prawn dumplings 132
stir-fried prawns with
pineapple and chilli
salad 231
tom yum goong 112
primavera, pasta 199
prosciutto, crisp, with
mango and avocado
salsa 24
prunes, stewed, with
orange 365

Q

quesadillas, spinach and
cheese 136

R

raspberry
and peach juice 80
crushed pavlovas with
honey yogurt and
mixed berries 386
mixed berries with
sponge fingers 373
mixed berry juice 47
summer berry stack 354
rice
artichoke risotto 203
curried pork stir-fry with
wild rice 326
garlic prawns and buk
choy with herbed rice
123
microwave prawn and
pea risotto 244
nasi goreng 192
thai chicken and rice 287
warm rice and chickpea
salad171
ricotta
baked ricotta with
tomato 15

(*ricotta* continued)
bruschetta with
strawberry, banana
and ricotta 36
panettone with ricotta
and caramelised
peaches 369

S

salade niçoise 179
salad
asian crispy noodle 160
balmain bugs and citrus
salad 275
beef and noodle 325
beef with green papaya,
chilli and coriander 152
caesar 144
cajun lamb backstraps
with four-bean salad
345
char-grilled chicken
with warm tomato
salad 308
char-grilled tuna 268
chicken and crunchy
noodle 147
chilli prawns, barbecued,
with fresh mango
salad 263
glazed-chicken tortilla
with sprout and herb
salad 292
green vegetable salad
with american mustard
dressing 176
grilled asparagus with
warm tomato dressing
184
harissa chicken with
couscous salad 300
japanese omelette 159
kiwi fruit, lychee and
lime 362
mexican bean salad with
tortilla chips 183
mixed bean salad 175
moroccan beef 322
pan fried tofu with
vietnamese coleslaw
151
panzanella 167
pearl barley 180
pepper-crusted swordfish
with bean and potato
salad 247
pickled green papaya 172

(*salad* continued)
poached flathead with
herb salad 216
potato and bean salad
with lemon yogurt
dressing 168
prawn, scallop and
asparagus salad with
ginger dressing 252
rice and chickpea salad,
warm 171
roasted egg tomatoes
with barley salad 163
salade niçoise 179
scallops with sugar snap
pea salad 271
shredded chicken 291
smoked chicken 188
soba and daikon 156
soba salad with
seaweed, ginger and
vegetables 187
stir-fried prawns with
pineapple and chilli
salad 231
sumac, salt and pepper
fish with mediterranean
salad 280
thai chicken 155
thai fish burgers with
sour and sweet green
salad 232
thai pork with kaffir lime
dressing 143
tuna and white bean 148
vietnamese chicken 140
white bean 164
sang choy bow 330
sashimi stacks 248
scallops
char-grilled scallops with
citrus salsa 223
grilled scallops with
papaya salsa 236
prawn, scallop and
asparagus salad with
ginger dressing 252
with sugar snap pea
salad 271
seafood
asian-flavoured trout
with shiitake mushrooms
264
balmain bugs and citrus
salad 276
calamari teppanyaki 224

(*seafood* continued)
fish with herb and
   tomato dressing 276
fish with thai-style
   dressing 255
grilled blue-eye with
   gai lan 267
pepper-crusted
   swordfish with bean
   and potato salad 247
poached flathead with
   herb salad 216
sashimi stacks 248
squid stuffed with
   smoked trout and
   basil 259
steamed mussels with
   saffron, chilli and
   coriander 228
stir-fried octopus with
   basil 240
sumac, salt and pepper
   fish with mediterranean
   salad 280
thai fish burgers with
   sour and sweet green
   salad 232
silverbeet
apple and celery juice 83
carrot, ginger and
   silverbeet juice 59
singapore noodles 200
smoked salmon and dill,
   scrambled eggs with 35
smoked salmon, cream
   cheese and rocket,
   bruschetta with 32
snapper
crisp-skinned snapper
   with stir-fried vegetables
   and black beans 260
grilled snapper with spicy
   tomato sauce 227
soba and daikon salad
   156
soba salad with seaweed,
   ginger and vegetables
   187
soufflés, passionfruit 378
soup
chicken pho 103
clear vegetable 100
curried chicken and
   zucchini 107
ginger vegetable and
   soba 111

(*soup* continued)
leek and potato 104
meatball pho 108
tom yum goong 112
spinach
and cheese quesadillas
   136
beetroot, carrot and
   spinach juice 60
poached eggs with
   bacon, spinach and
   pecorino 28
squid stuffed with smoked
   trout and basil 259
strawberry
and papaya juice 84
bruschetta with
   strawberry, banana
   and ricotta 36
crushed pavlovas with
   honey yogurt and
   mixed berries 386
honey and soy smoothie
   95
hotcakes with blueberry
   sauce 16
mixed berry juice 47
morning trifles 27
orange, mango and
   strawberry juice 88
peach, apple and
   strawberry juice 44
pineapple, orange and
   strawberry juice 75
summer berry stack 354
sukiyaki, vegetarian 211
sumac, salt and pepper
   fish with mediterranean
   salad 280
summer berry stack 354
sweet chilli prawn
   dumplings, steamed
   132
swordfish, pepper-crusted,
   with bean and potato
   salad 247
T
tandoori pockets, chicken,
   with raita 127
tangelo and ginger juice 52
teriyaki lamb stir-fry 334
thai chicken and rice 288
thai chicken salad 155
thai fish burgers with
   sour and sweet green
   salad 232

thai pork salad with kaffir
   lime dressing 143
tofu, pan-fried, with
   vietnamese coleslaw
   salad 151
tofu, stir-fried, with
   vegetables and lemon
   grass 212
tom yum goong 112
tomato
baked ricotta with
   tomato 15
breakfast with the lot 20
char-grilled chicken
   with warm tomato
   salad 308
cucumber and tomato
   salsa 312
egg-white omelette 39
fish with herb and tomato
   dressing 276
grilled snapper with spicy
   tomato sauce 227
roasted egg tomatoes
   with barley salad 163
trifles, morning 27
tropical fruit skewers with
   coconut dressing 370
tuna
and white bean salad 148
char-grilled tuna salad
   268
japanese-style tuna with
   red-maple radish 219
salade niçoise 179
seared tuna with chilled
   soba 251
V
veal and fettuccine in sage
   mustard sauce 346
veal cutlets with brussel
   sprouts and celeriac
   mash 341
vegetable soup, clear 100
vegetable stacks,
   roasted 207
vegetable stir-fry 204
vegetarian sukiyaki 211
vietnamese chicken
   salad 140
W
watercress, beetroot and
   celery juice 55
watermelon and
   mint juice 56
white bean salad 164

MEASURES

One Australian metric measuring cup holds approximately 250ml, one Australian metric tablespoon holds 20ml, one Australian metric teaspoon holds 5ml.

The difference between one country's measuring cups and another's is within a two- or three-teaspoon variance, and will not affect your cooking results.North America, New Zealand and the United Kingdom use a 15ml tablespoon.

All cup and spoon measurements are level. The most accurate way of measuring dry ingredients is to weigh them. When measuring liquids, use a clear glass or plastic jug with the metric markings.

We use large eggs with an average weight of 60g.

LIQUID MEASURES

METRIC	IMPERIAL
30ml	1 fluid oz
60ml	2 fluid oz
100ml	3 fluid oz
125ml	4 fluid oz
150ml	5 fluid oz (¼ pint/1 gill)
190ml	6 fluid oz
250ml	8 fluid oz
300ml	10 fluid oz (½ pint)
500ml	16 fluid oz
600ml	20 fluid oz (1 pint)
1000ml (1 litre)	1¾ pints

LENGTH MEASURES

METRIC	IMPERIAL
3mm	⅛in
6mm	¼in
1cm	½in
2cm	¾in
2.5cm	1in
5cm	2in
6cm	2½in
8cm	3in
10cm	4in
13cm	5in
15cm	6in
18cm	7in
20cm	8in
23cm	9in
25cm	10in
28cm	11in
30cm	12in (1ft)

DRY MEASURES

METRIC	IMPERIAL
15g	½oz
30g	1oz
60g	2oz
90g	3oz
125g	4oz (¼lb)
155g	5oz
185g	6oz
220g	7oz
250g	8oz (½lb)
280g	9oz
315g	10oz
345g	11oz
375g	12oz (¾lb)
410g	13oz
440g	14oz
470g	15oz
500g	16oz (1lb)
750g	24oz (1½lb)
1kg	32oz (2lb)

OVEN TEMPERATURES

These oven temperatures are only a guide for conventional ovens.
For fan-forced ovens, check the manufacturer's manual.

	°C (CELSIUS)	°F (FAHRENHEIT)	GAS MARK
Very slow	120	250	½
Slow	150	275 – 300	1 – 2
Moderately slow	160	325	3
Moderate	180	350 – 375	4 – 5
Moderately hot	200	400	6
Hot	220	425 – 450	7 – 8
Very hot	240	475	9

General manager Christine Whiston
Editorial director Susan Tomnay
Creative director Hieu Chi Nguyen
Senior editor Stephanie Kistner
Designer Caryl Wiggins
Food director Pamela Clark
Recipe consultant Louise Patniotis
Nutritional information Rebecca Squadrito
Director of sales Brian Cearnes
Marketing manager Bridget Cody
Business analyst Rebecca Varela
Operations manager David Scotto
Production manager Victoria Jefferys
International rights enquiries Laura Bamford
lbamford@acpuk.com

ACP Books are published by ACP Magazines
a division of PBL Media Pty Limited
Group publisher, Women's lifestyle Pat Ingram
Director of sales, Women's lifestyle Lynette Phillips
Commercial manager, Women's lifestyle Seymour Cohen
Marketing director, Women's lifestyle Matthew Dominello
Public relations manager, Women's lifestyle Hannah Deveraux
Creative director, Events, Women's lifestyle Luke Bonnano
Research Director, Women's lifestyle Justin Stone
ACP Magazines, Chief Executive officer Scott Lorson
PBL Media, Chief Executive officer Ian Law

Produced by ACP Books, Sydney.
Published by ACP Books, a division of ACP Magazines Ltd.
54 Park St, Sydney NSW Australia 2000. GPO Box 4088, Sydney, NSW 2001.
Phone +61 2 9282 8618 Fax +61 2 9267 9438
acpbooks@acpmagazines.com.au www.acpbooks.com.au
Printed by Toppan Printing Co., China.

Australia Distributed by Network Services, GPO Box 4088, Sydney, NSW 2001.
Phone +61 2 9282 8777 Fax +61 2 9264 3278
networkweb@networkservicescompany.com.au
United Kingdom Distributed by Australian Consolidated Press (UK),
10 Scirocco Close, Moulton Park Office Village, Northampton, NN3 6AP.
Phone +44 1604 642 200 Fax +44 1604 642 300
books@acpuk.com www.acpuk.com
New Zealand Distributed by Netlink Distribution Company, ACP Media Centre,
Cnr Fanshawe and Beaumont Streets, Westhaven, Auckland. PO Box 47906, Ponsonby, Auckland, NZ.
Phone +64 9 366 9966 Fax 0800 277 412 ask@ndc.co.nz
South Africa Distributed by PSD Promotions, 30 Diesel Road Isando, Gauteng Johannesburg.
PO Box 1175, Isando 1600, Gauteng Johannesburg.
Phone +27 11 392 6065/6/7 Fax +27 11 392 6079/80 orders@psdprom.co.za
Canada Distributed by Publishers Group Canada
Order Desk & Customer Service 9050 Shaughnessy Street, Vancouver BC V6P 6E5
Phone (800) 663 5714 Fax (800) 565 3770 service@raincoast.com

Clark, Pamela.
The Australian Women's Weekly fast healthy
ISBN 978-1-86396-602-3
1. Cookery (Natural foods).
I. Title. II Title: Australian women's weekly.
641.563
© ACP Magazines Ltd 2007
ABN 18 053 273 546
This publication is copyright. No part of it may be reproduced or
transmitted in any form without the written permission of the publishers.
First published 2007. Reprinted 2008.

To order books, phone 136 116 (within Australia).
Send recipe enquiries to: askpamela@acpmagazines.com.au

Cover Spinach quesadillas, page 136
Photographer Ian Wallace
Stylist Sarah O'Brien
Additional photography Chris Chen
Additional styling Stephanie Souvlis
Food preparation Nicole Jennings